WITHDRAWN

SCHOOLS COUNCIL

Mixed-ability teaching in mathematics

a survey of current practice prepared
by the Schools Council Working Group
on Mixed-ability Teaching in Mathematics

Evans/Methuen Educational

First published 1977 for the Schools Council
by Evans Brothers Limited
Montague House, Russell Square, London WC1B 5BX
and Methuen Educational
11 New Fetter Lane, London EC4P 4EE

© *Schools Council Publications 1977*

ISBN 0 423 89940 6

IBM set by Jubal Multiwrite Limited, London SE13
and printed in Great Britain by
Unwin Brothers Limited
The Gresham Press, Old Woking, Surrey

Contents

Foreword   *page* 7

Preface   9

Part 1. Mixed-ability grouping: characteristics and current practice   11

I   Mixed-ability grouping: the background   13
Types of teaching group   13
Grouping by ability   14
Mixed-ability grouping   16
Teaching mixed-ability classes   17

II   Mathematics teaching   19
Aims of mathematics teaching   19
Mathematical learning   20
Characteristics of good mathematics teaching   20

III Mathematics and mixed-ability grouping   27
The nature of mathematics   27
Changing views of mathematics   28
Variation in pupils' attainment   29
Demands on the teacher   30
Design of suitable materials   30

IV   Some teaching models and current practices   32
Teaching models   32
Exercises and exploratory tasks   35
The relationship between teaching models, exercises and exploratory
tasks   36
A comparison of different teaching models   37
Classroom practice   40
Summary   48

V **Results of the inquiry and recommendations**   50
   Findings   50
   Recommendations   62

   References and notes   65

   Part 2. Mixed-ability teaching in action   67

VI **The working group's inquiry**   69
    Questions put to teachers   69
    Observations in the classroom   74

VII **Three case studies**   78
     School A   78
     School B   96
     School C   105

VIII **Materials in use**   130

      Acknowledgements   143

      Members of the working group   146

Foreword

Mixed-ability teaching is viewed by some mathematics teachers as a challenge, by others as a threat; but all are agreed that its adoption calls for a reappraisal of classroom organization, teaching methods and materials. With the decision of many secondary and middle schools to move towards mixed-ability grouping, finding effective ways of putting it into practice has become a major preoccupation of teachers of mathematics.

The Schools Council includes among its functions those of undertaking inquiries, offering advice to schools and preparing and publishing reports on its activities. Its Mathematics Committee, whose members cover between them a wide range of interests at all levels of mathematical education, felt that it could most effectively help teachers faced with the problem of implementing mixed-ability teaching by establishing a working group which would identify and visit schools in which this kind of organization was working well and by making its findings available as quickly as possible. Whatever the views held by individual committee members on the desirability of mixed-ability grouping, we are unanimous in our concern that, where it is undertaken, every pupil should receive from it the best possible mathematical training.

One especially happy feature of this exercise has been the close collaboration between the Schools Council and two subject teaching associations – the Mathematical Association and the Association of Teachers of Mathematics. Several members representing each association were active members of the group, bringing to the inquiry invaluable knowledge and experience.

I congratulate the working group on the spirit in which it undertook its task, and warmly commend its report to all who care for the health of mathematics teaching in this country.

Douglas Quadling
Chairman
Schools Council Mathematics Committee
1973–77

Preface

Members of the Schools Council Mathematics Committee have been increasingly concerned with calls for advice on and assistance with mixed-ability teaching from colleagues throughout the country. As a result, the committee decided in 1975 to initiate an investigation into current practice in mixed-ability teaching in mathematics in a variety of schools, albeit limited in number, in order to report on what it considered to be examples of good practice and to offer help to those teachers who wanted it.

The committee therefore appointed a working group consisting of a number of their own members together with people of experience from the Mathematical Association, the Association of Teachers of Mathematics and the National Foundation for Educational Research (members of the group are listed at the end of this report). In 1976 P. A. Bailey (an experienced head of department in a comprehensive school) was seconded as secretary/writer to the group to spearhead the one-year survey and write the report. He was supported on his visits to schools by various members of the working group, some of whom were convinced exponents of mixed-ability teaching while others were quite otherwise!

The result of the working group's inquiry is a document which does not set out to be 'evangelistic' in character. We are not concerned to win converts as such. We have, however, attempted to produce a survey from which we hope teachers will be able to derive encouragement and glean relevant information and fresh insight. We hope it will help them to reappraise their local situation and perhaps initiate moves to improve their own performance and expertise.*

It would not be surprising if many readers gave their first attention to Chapter V, where the results of the survey are presented. We would draw special attention also to the wealth of detailed information in the case studies (Chapter VII) and the review of teaching materials (Chapter VIII). However, the report is to be seen as a whole and we would sincerely hope that colleagues will wish to read all of it in order to set the practical findings within the framework of the

---

* The working group has also prepared a discussion pack on mixed-ability teaching in mathematics (containing slides, a cassette tape commentary and additional discussion sheets) for use in in-service training, conferences, lectures, etc.

theoretical considerations advanced. The interaction between aims, objectives, practices and outcomes may then be seen more clearly.

The Mathematics Committee would appreciate feedback from the profession and hope that teachers, in facing up to both the problems and opportunities that mixed-ability teaching brings, will find not only a stimulus to their own work but a *modus operandi* that is soundly based and educationally productive in meeting the needs and demands of pupils, parents and employers.

R. T. Richardson
Chairman, Schools Council Working Group
on Mixed-ability Teaching in Mathematics

Part 1

Mixed-ability grouping: characteristics and current practice

I. Mixed-ability grouping: the background

TYPES OF TEACHING GROUP

There are many ways of arranging pupils in classes, of which the four most common are:

Streaming
The division of pupils into classes on the basis of general ability and/or attainment, the classes then remaining the same for all subjects.

Setting
A whole or part of a year group is timetabled as a block; pupils are then divided on the basis of attainment within each subject.

Banding
A year group is divided into a number of broad streams on the basis of attainment. Wide-ability classes or else classes within which there is assumed to be a similar range of ability can then be formed within each band.

Mixed-ability grouping
Classes are formed covering the full ability range, roughly matching that found in the population of the school. Such classes may have the least able pupils removed for some or all of the time. (Since any group of pupils will constitute a 'mixed-ability group' a better term might be 'all-ability group'.)

Mixed-ability grouping has increasingly been adopted by comprehensive schools, but opinions continue to vary as to its effectiveness. Proponents see mixed-ability grouping as having great social, practical and educational benefits but others, while agreeing that gifted and enthusiastic teachers working in this way may achieve success, fear that those not so committed to the underlying philosophy will be less successful.

Many teachers feel that some form of grouping by ability or attainment will lead to better academic progress by pupils. Such research as has been done (mostly in the USA, or in primary schools in the UK) has been largely concerned with streaming rather than setting, and shows no definite advantage for academic standards from either homogeneous or heterogeneous classes.[1,2,3,4] In both streamed and non-streamed classes there appears to be a danger of a self-verifying hypothesis related to teacher expectation,[5] which in streamed classes sometimes leads to under-achievement among the less able, and in mixed-ability classes may result in the ablest children not being extended.[6,7] The one conclusion that has been demonstrated beyond reasonable doubt is that the form of grouping is less important than the many other variables present in the classroom — the teacher, teaching methods, the age range of the pupils, the subject taught, class size, the degree of streaming and whether or not remedial children are included in mixed-ability classes, the brevity of the experiment and the Hawthorne effect,[8] and the general school ethos.*

It is not the purpose of this report to suggest that mixed-ability grouping is the 'right' way to teach mathematics, but a brief account of the development of the various types of grouping and of the arguments advanced for and against them may help teachers to consider the possibilities.

GROUPING BY ABILITY

The development of streaming and setting

Streaming developed in the 1920s and 1930s as techniques for mental testing were devised to separate children into classes of about the same ability level. The Hadow Report[9] recommended 'triple track' ability grouping in those primary schools with enough pupils of the same age. Further endorsement of streaming was given by the Spens Report,[10] and the Norwood Report,[11] which introduced the concept of different types of children needing different types of school.

Learning theory between the wars was dominated by the views of Cyril Burt,[12] who regarded intelligence as:

> ... inherited, or at least innate, not due to teaching or training; it is intellectual, not emotional or moral, and remains uninfluenced by industry or zeal; it is general, not specific ... (pp. 28–9)

*Further research in this field has been undertaken by the Department of Education and Science. For a report of the project, see D. Newbold, *Ability Grouping: the Banbury Enquiry* (National Foundation for Educational Research, Slough, 1977).

14

Tests were devised to measure intelligence and thus to label a pupil for the purpose of selection and streaming.

Streaming was regarded as being of great benefit to all pupils. It was seen as a means of nurturing the talents of bright children on the educational ladder to university and helping the less able child, since he could be given special attention. Setting for a particular subject was similarly intended to optimize conditions for learning by enabling pupils to work at an appropriate level and pace with others of a similar standard.

Arguments in favour of setting

In many subjects there is a considerable spread of ability and attainment and many teachers argued that:

> pupils at the extremes of the range require different approaches, even different courses;

> a setted group lends itself to 'whole-class' teaching;

> different examinations imposed different syllabuses on different pupils, making setting desirable.

Doubts about streaming and setting

The idea that a child's intelligence is fixed and easily measured had long been questioned by some. In the 1950s and 1960s a more dynamic view of intelligence as ' . . . a highly complex and fluid collection of skills . . . greatly influenced by a person's total experience . . .' developed.[13] This view of intelligence led to the following questions being asked:

> Is inherited intelligence the most important factor in academic success?

> Can latent ability be measured and used for selection?

> Can intelligence be developed through the use of language, enriched environment and interaction with adults?

Teachers became aware of error and bias in the actual selection process. For example, it was found that autumn born children score more highly on intelligence tests than summer born children [14,15] and more girls were found to be in the top streams than might be expected.[3] The effects of environmental deprivation and family size became apparent, as did the streaming of teachers — the tendency for the most able teachers to teach the best classes.

Social effects of streaming and setting

In contrast to the inconclusive findings about academic attainment already mentioned, research into the social outcomes of grouping by ability has been more positive:

streaming was a self-verifying hypothesis related to teacher expectation,[5] artificially widening the gap between the least and most able;[6]

a false impression of homogeneity in the class limited the learning opportunities presented;

streaming reinforced the process of social selection, was significantly related to social class, and reflected social background and parental aspiration;[16]

in streamed schools sub-cultures developed — the academic and the anti-academic;[17]

segregation grouped together awkward pupils in lower streams, helping to create delinquent groups, anti-social and anti-teacher;[18,19]

the rigidity of the system was reflected in the very limited movement of pupils between sets.

MIXED-ABILITY GROUPING

As well as accepting the arguments leading them to reject streaming and setting, teachers adopting mixed-ability grouping hoped to gain more opportunities:

for curriculum development;

to meet the needs of individual pupils;

for co-operative planning and team-work;

16

to develop the self-esteem of all pupils;

to improve teacher—pupil relationships;

for the more flexible use of available resources.

TEACHING MIXED-ABILITY CLASSES

The main concern of schools that have adopted this approach is how to develop methods of teaching that are suitable for mixed-ability classes. It is important to appreciate that, whatever type of grouping is chosen, it is the philosophy, attitudes and responsiveness of the teacher that are important; good classroom practice depends much more on the teacher than on the particular grouping adopted.

A mixed-ability class can be taught in a variety of ways, but good teaching will focus on the needs of the individual pupil and will not be based on an assumption that every member of the class will learn a topic at the same time or at the same rate. There will, of course, be a spread of ability in any class, even in a setted situation, so that methods that are particularly appropriate to a class with a wide range of ability can be used elsewhere. When dealing with a wide range of ability the teacher must be more than ever concerned to:

provide a common core for the full range of ability;

provide tasks which will stretch all pupils academically;

provide material that will interest the full ability range;

ensure that all students work hard;

help children with a low level of basic skills;

assess work at many different levels;

monitor the progress of each pupil.

A school or department about to adopt mixed-ability teaching must take into account:

the changing demands on teachers, both inside and outside the classroom;

the need to provide in-service support for teachers inexperienced in mixed-ability teaching;

the attitudes of parents and employers;

the range, organization and deployment of resources;

the balance to be achieved between published courses and locally produced material;

the work involved in producing and developing resources within the school.

The defenders of mixed-ability teaching would argue that the aims of mathematics teaching can be at least as well served in mixed-ability groups as with any other type of organization. This claim is discussed, in the light of both theory and of practice as the working group found it, in this report. Later chapters examine how mathematics teachers have tried to achieve, in mixed-ability classes, the aims and objectives outlined above, and the extent to which they have succeeded.

II. Mathematics teaching

In considering methods of teaching mathematics in mixed-ability classes it is necessary to review the general aims of mathematics teaching, the different aspects of mathematical learning and the general properties of good mathematics teaching.

AIMS OF MATHEMATICS TEACHING

We have taken mathematics to be firstly a means of gaining a particular insight into the environment. The form of growth function of populations, the ways of turning a mattress, the concept of acceleration, the concept of the decrease in the rate of inflation and the correct understanding of the statistical 'law of averages' are everyday examples, and any occupational or leisure situation will furnish many more. Secondly, the general attraction of puzzles and patterns, and the existence of amateur number theorists, suggest that the capacity to appreciate mathematics as an art to be enjoyed is also present in many people. These two perceptions of mathematics correspond to the applied and the pure approaches and they have been identified throughout history as the mainsprings of mathematical activity.

The aims and objectives of mathematics teaching have changed over the course of time. This has happened in response to the changing needs of society and to a deepening understanding of what can be learned and retained so as to influence a pupil's capabilities after he has left school. Until recently the only mathematical education for nearly all pupils was an intensive training in computations with money, weights and measures, and fractions. This was achieved with considerable repetition and was cumulative in that the simpler processes were component parts of the more advanced. We know from reports by H M Inspectorate that there was a good deal of rote learning in the syllabus and that it produced a very low level of mathematical understanding. The development of the curriculum, bringing in geometry, trigonometry, graphical work and algebra, took place partly in response to industrial needs — no industrial apprentice today would find computation to be all that he requires — and partly because these wider subjects were thought to be interesting, enlightening and accessible to most of the pupils concerned. More recently statistics has been introduced into the school curriculum for similar reasons.

MATHEMATICAL LEARNING

We can classify what is to be learned in mathematics into:

Skills
Concepts
Relationships
Strategies.

Skills are the operational aspects of performance, such as converting vulgar fractions to percentages or decimals, identifying the symmetries of a given solid, finding the distance between two points whose co-ordinates are given, drawing the graph of a given equation. All of these can be taught as unconnected routines and practised until sufficient accuracy is achieved.

Concepts are generalizations such as fraction, percentage, decimal, symmetry, solid, distance, point, co-ordinate, graph, equation.

Relationships are the links between lower-order concepts, for example the relationship between the area of any surface and its dimensions, or the projective relationships between different conic sections. The importance of relationships lies in the fact that unconnected skills and concepts may fade away relatively quickly, whereas well-connected bodies of skills are very much better retained. Relationships are acquired through problems and investigations — indeed, solving a problem essentially means establishing a connection between aspects of a situation not previously connected.

Strategies are groups of skills selected to deal with whole classes of situations. Examples are proof strategies (the identification of data and conclusions, and the organization of the argument connecting them), generalization strategies (the generation of further relevant examples, the making of a conjecture, the search for a general argument), and 'fall back' strategies (recourse to concrete material or a familiar structured situation when stuck on a problem). Strategies are acquired through experience of the relevant activity, preferably with subsequent reflection on, and discussion of, significant aspects of the process.

These four categories should not be thought of as hierarchically linked in the learning process, but they are to a large extent interactive.

CHARACTERISTICS OF GOOD MATHEMATICS TEACHING

The following headings were used as a basis for discussion with teachers during the course of this survey. They are suggested as desirable aspects of all good mathematics teaching.

Quality
(a)   Sound mathematical content and variety of tasks.
(b)   Suitability of tasks for pupils (appropriate level of difficulty, interest and relevance).

Continuity
(a)   Continuity and development of the mathematical learning of individual pupils.
(b)   Awareness by the teacher of individual pupils' progress.

Autonomy
Development of the pupil's ability to organize his own learning activities.

Discussion
Mathematical discussion between pupils and between teacher and pupil.

Quality

'Quality' does not necessarily imply a commercial standard of production but, rather, tasks which will ensure that concepts or relationships are formed or used with strategies in developing mathematical activity; such tasks should offer plenty of scope for the pupil's development in a variety of classroom situations (e.g. class/group/individual). Neither does variety necessarily imply pupil choice. When choice is offered this must be done in such a way that pupils can make appropriate choices.

Continuity

To ensure continuity the teacher must be aware of the structure of the mathematical course and of the progress of individual pupils.

(a) The structure of the course

Links between topics. In conventional class teaching the teacher will relate a new topic to earlier work, picking up the threads through preliminary references and questions, and showing other links as the topic develops. A more individualized scheme can include early references in some of the first sections

21

or cards, but as pupils may study parts of the course in different orders, further links must be carefully arranged. One approach is to link the tasks and topics by a flowchart as in the School Mathematics Project (SMP) work cards scheme, the Kent Mathematics Project (KMP) and the Secondary Mathematics Individualized Learning Experiment (SMILE).*

In such a scheme, continuity may be broken through three factors: the teacher, the way the scheme is operated, a pupil's lack of understanding. If the teacher is under pressure or unfamiliar with the scheme he may direct the pupil to a card or worksheet which is not related to the tasks already completed. As the teacher becomes more familiar with the structure of the scheme this is less likely to happen.

Some schools have developed schemes with a high degree of pupil choice. There are advantages to be gained by offering pupils such freedom, but there are risks as well. With a free choice, do pupils naturally choose a topic which develops their previous knowledge? With schemes that incorporate pupil choice there is an argument for designing a set of tasks which is at least loosely structured. Teacher guidance is an important factor in maintaining continuity where pupil choice exists, because without it there are likely to be serious breaks in continuity. A hidden structure behind the free choice of tasks ensures that pupils do not choose unsuitable topics and ensures coverage of essential sections.

Any scheme involving pupil or teacher choice implies that different pupils will tackle the various topics in different orders. A linear scheme, in which all pupils proceed through the topics in the same order, has the advantage that a pupil 'picks up' a theme later at the point where he left it; the progression through the scheme ensures continuity. A disadvantage of such schemes is that the less able can get bogged down and become disheartened. The introduction of some element of choice can help to minimize this effect and is a good motivating factor in any scheme.

Continuity within topics. With an individualized system using either a book or work cards, a pupil can pick up where he left off the previous lesson. This can be a very effective method. However, if different pupils have reached different stages in the topic and the teacher leads every lesson, his comments will not be wholly appropriate to all the class and he may break pupils' lines of thinking, rather than aiding continuity. In addition, the teacher may introduce a 'cut off' before a pupil has achieved the objective of a particular topic.

If work cards or books are to be used as the sole basis for learning, very full explanations must be incorporated in the materials if continuity is to be achieved, but because they are then self-contained the tendency will be for less teacher back-

*The materials referred to here are described more fully in Chapter VIII.

up and communication between teacher and pupil. Thus, although the teacher may have checked off a number of work cards or tests, he may still be aware neither of the nature of the pupil's difficulties nor of his actual achievement. A well-designed course builds on a pupil's earlier knowledge and breaks down if he has failed to understand properly a task which he has completed, apparently successfully. To prevent this happening the teacher must monitor the pupil's progress, assessing his understanding by discussion and testing.

(b) Awareness of pupils' progress

Assessment is the means by which a teacher becomes aware of a pupil's progress. Most teachers use a mixture of formal and informal assessment.

Informal assessment relies very heavily on teacher—pupil discussion. By questioning the pupil on what he has done the teacher is able to test his understanding and diagnose his difficulties. This type of assessment, if used without some formal recording, can be unreliable when used to direct the pupil to a new task. Without a formal record it may be difficult to decide at which point the pupil should enter the topic (the pupil may even have already done the task some time ago) and some formal record is necessary to pass on to the pupil's next teacher. A 'pupil profile' can be used to show particular strengths and achievements in detail.

Many teachers would argue that formal assessment too easily becomes assessment of those aspects of learning that can be readily assessed in a formal way, and that some aspects can only be effectively assessed informally; a blend of the two approaches is therefore necessary. A further danger of formal assessment is that the teacher can easily become bogged down in administration. Consider, for example, a system which involves the pupils working through a linear sequence of topic booklets: when a pupil has completed a booklet the teacher marks it and then gives him a test sheet on that topic. The teacher marks the test sheet; if the pupil performs badly on the test he has to repeat it, after further explanation by the teacher. When the test sheet has been satisfactorily completed the teacher then directs the pupil to the next topic booklet. With such a system it is not difficult to imagine a long queue forming at the teacher's desk.

Recording progress. It is useful to have marks or a grading system for topics, although this may not reveal everything about a pupil's performance in that topic. Assessments range from a simple tick to interviews where the teacher asks careful questions of an open-ended kind which reveal a pupil's understanding of a topic. Such interviews also enable the *pupil* to clarify ideas on points about which he was confused, and to appreciate the state of his own understanding; but detailed questioning and discussion are necessary if the interviews are to be really effective.

Another type of assessment procedure that includes brief interviews is called the CUSP method (see Fig. 1). This is a simple system of marking, assessment and record-keeping which ensures that the purpose of the task has been understood and tries to develop standards of presentation and neatness. Apart from checking answers, the teacher assesses the work impressionistically with regard to presentation, understanding and application of techniques, perseverance, creativity, and the ability to derive suitable conclusions. The full assessment necessitates a brief interview with the pupil to assess his understanding of the task and to give him a chance to ask questions. The teacher uses this opportunity to encourage the pupil and each pupil is required to keep his own record of the tasks he has completed. A system is used in which the approximate percentage of the year group which will achieve each grade is as follows (a five-point scale is applied to the whole year group):

		per cent
Grade A	(excellent)	5
Grade B	(good)	20
Grade C	(average)	50
Grade D	(below average)	20
Grade E	(weak)	5

Pupil	Topic								
	Slide rule 1					Slide rule 2			
Sharon	√	B	A	A		√	A	A	B
David	✗	C	D	D					
Assessment	C	U	S	P		C	U	S	P

C – topic completed (√ or ✗)
U – understanding (oral assessment) (A–E)
S – overall standard or quality of work (A–E)
P – presentation and neatness (A–E)

Fig. 1 Teacher's record for the CUSP method of assessment

Autonomy

To develop a pupil's autonomy the teacher may encourage him to organize his own materials, assessment or tasks. Besides the obvious aim of encouraging the pupil to become self-reliant and to take initiatives when appropriate, the demands on the teacher can be eased in this way, so that he is available to help pupils with problems, to teach small groups or individuals, or to deal with matters of discipline. The pupil can be given the responsibility of marking his own course-work. This self-assessment can be backed up by interviews with the teacher or by some form of post-test administered by the teacher.

In some individualized schemes the pupil has a choice of tasks, and is usually guided directly or indirectly by the teacher, the scheme or other pupils. Discussion and guidance minimize the danger of a pupil choosing a totally unsuitable task. When working in a small group the members of that group have to make decisions about strategies and 'write-ups'; these decisions about the way the task is to be attempted can only be reached by discussion. Discussion is important in investigative work whether this is carried out in groups or individually. The pupil has to organize himself in such a way that he explores situations which are useful, and the ability to distinguish useful avenues of investigation can only be acquired gradually. Some guided discovery may be essential before the pupil becomes more self-reliant.

Pupils' independence can be encouraged by a variety of approaches. For example, a workshop scheme with a choice of tasks in the form of topic booklets offers the opportunity for the pupil to pursue his own interests. Obviously the teacher can control the activities to some degree by the variety of booklets he puts on offer.

Whatever the system, and however well it encourages pupil autonomy, the teacher must develop the skill to know when and where to intervene. Near the end of a lesson he may make a deliberate attempt to see all the pupils he has not already contacted during the lesson. In this way he can monitor each pupil's own organization and offer advice when necessary.

Discussion

Discussion can be a very powerful and effective agent in promoting good teaching and should be used for purposes other than the common ones of administration, assessment and assistance.

Teacher–pupil discussion

This form of exchange provides the teacher with information, helps him to collect ideas for supplementary work and extensions of a topic, and helps him to assess the suitability of a task or its presentation.

Discussion plays a part at three stages in the development of a sequence of work.

i   Introducing the topic, situation or theme: helping pupils to form links with earlier work; explaining the topic; giving instructions.

ii Developing the work: suggestions for the next step; clarification of the pupils' ideas; extensions (for example, in unusual situations); valid generalizations; assistance.

iii Concluding the work: bringing out the significance of what has been done and deciding on follow-up tasks or more work to consolidate what has been done already.

These discussions may be on a class basis or with individual pupils and can help the teacher to ensure that the topic has been brought to a satisfactory state of completion.

Pupil–pupil discussion

Discussion between pupils is also of value. It can provide them with information, consolidate their knowledge, help them to choose appropriate skills, develop strategies, and compare the results of an investigation.

In this chapter, the aims of teaching mathematics, aspects of mathematical learning and a number of requirements for good mathematics teaching have been considered. The way in which these considerations are affected by mixed-ability grouping are described in Chapter III.

III. Mathematics and mixed-ability grouping

This chapter brings together the two strands considered so far – mixed-ability grouping and the requirements of mathematics teaching – and seeks to relate the one to the other.

THE NATURE OF MATHEMATICS

Mathematics is frequently regarded as a subject which does not lend itself readily to mixed-ability teaching. A report on a survey conducted by the Assistant Masters' Association states: [20]

> It was significant that mathematics teachers in secondary schools were more reluctant than other specialists to adapt their approach and methodology to the needs of mixed-ability groups. (p. 24)

The usual reasons for making mathematics a special case lie in the perceived structure of the subject, the way it is taught, the differences of attainment that exist among pupils of the same age, and the different levels of understanding that an individual may have within the subject. It has been argued that the nature of mathematics makes it impossible, or very difficult, to teach to mixed-ability groups, since it is a highly structured, linear progression or hierarchy of concepts as described, for example, by Skemp.[21] Each step has to be understood and mastered before the pupil proceeds to the next. A teacher with a homogeneous class could vary the rate of progress so as to ensure the mastery of each step by all.

In this context, however, it must be said that the linear progression of concepts is used to develop courses with a high proportion of individualized learning for mixed-ability classes. Collaborative efforts such as the School Mathematics Individualized Learning Experiment and the Kent Mathematics Project have developed banks of materials based on a linear progression of topics and parallel tasks.* Some schools have developed their own courses based on the philosophy described by Prettyman: [22]

*For a more detailed description of materials, see Chapter VIII.

27

The structure of the subject can be used to help the process of learning by breaking the structure down into basic concepts and building it up in the child's mind by a series of small but definite steps, like building-bricks or in a flow diagram . . . (p. 154)

An added advantage of an individualized course is that when a pupil returns from an absence he can pick up his work where he left off.[23] A linear view of mathematics, as described by Lingard:[24]

. . . presupposes that there is a certain clearly defined body of subject material which is important and has to be dispensed, in a particular order, to pupils . . . (p. 122)

However, in practice it has also proved possible to develop topic-based courses where there is variation in the order in which different pupils in the same class study the various topics.[25] Examples would include the SMP materials and those from the Resources for Learning Development Unit (RFLDU).

CHANGING VIEWS OF MATHEMATICS

The ideas of 'modern' mathematics have led to a re-evaluation of mathematical education. Recent developments have emphasized that mathematics is an activity as well as a body of knowledge to be mastered. More teachers have realized that:

Most children can appreciate, understand and enjoy the abstractions of mathematics more easily when they are given practical as well as theoretical significance. Many of the practical activities which teachers associate with maths — surveying, statistical research, mapwork, model-making — are well suited to group work and to work with children of mixed ability.[26]

Mathematical activities, investigations and starting-points designed to en-courage pupils to use concepts, often in unusual situations, have been developed by teachers. These opportunities have been used successfully by children in mixed-ability classes working individually, in groups, or as a class.[27, 28, 29, 30] Such departures from the conventional lesson have increased pupils' interest in and enjoyment of mathematics.

VARIATION IN PUPILS' ATTAINMENT

As mathematics develops it becomes more abstract and there is a considerable variation both in the time taken for pupils to build up more abstract concepts from a number of particular examples, and in the level of abstraction at which pupils can work. In a mixed-ability class the presence of a wide range of achievement complicates the provision of content, allocation of tasks, assessment and homework.

Since each pupil will have different abilities and levels of understanding *within* the subject, they are unlikely to have the same aptitudes. All pupils in a setted class do not reach the same level of understanding at the same time, as any teacher of such a class will confirm.

Research seems to suggest that there is no definite evidence about the degree of homogeneity required to teach particular subjects successfully,[31] but whatever type of class organization is used, the teaching methods must take account of the different levels of achievement within the class, so that a pupil's difficulties are diagnosed and his course consequently arranged to promote his mathematical development. For example, the correct balance between practical and abstract work must be achieved for each pupil. This decision, and others like it, depend on the teacher and the individual pupil and must be made whatever type of class grouping is used. In a setted situation the teacher tends to make these decisions for the class as a whole. Many teachers claim that the knowledge of individual pupils gained by the teacher in a mixed-ability class helps him to guide each pupil more reliably.

The most and the least able

The needs of pupils at the extremes of the ability spectrum must always be carefully considered. Many teachers feel that in a mixed-ability class it will be difficult to cater for both the most and the least able pupils so as to provide them with an appropriate challenge that will help them to develop their talents effectively. There is no evidence available to suggest that mixed-ability grouping does more than highlight what is everywhere a problem in this respect. Once such pupils have been identified, appropriate tasks can be given to them to further their development. Without minimizing the teaching skills required to do this it can be argued that mixed-ability grouping, especially in the early years of a secondary school, may enable 'late developers', for example, to be recognized and encouraged, and give those who have had a poor start the opportunity to catch up.

DEMANDS ON THE TEACHER

Successful mixed-ability teaching in mathematics demands much of the teacher in terms of organization and teaching skills. Since for most mathematics teachers radical changes of approach and teaching style are involved, mixed-ability teaching in mathematics must be approached carefully. In adopting this kind of grouping the teacher must rethink his strategy and role in the classroom, be prepared to innovate, be able to present and deal with a variety of activities in his classroom and be able to evaluate the success or failure of his work. Mixed-ability teaching inevitably demands detailed initial planning by all members of the mathematics department, and constant reassessment of their work. This kind of review offers the opportunity for teachers to improve their professional skills both inside and outside the classroom.

DESIGN OF SUITABLE MATERIALS

At first sight it would appear that the provision of material for mixed-ability classes might present insuperable problems relating to the continuity of experience for the individual pupil. It is necessary to design a topic so that pupils reaching very different end-points in their work on earlier sections can still profit from later developments of the topic without handicap. However, the writers of courses have always had to cope with this problem to some extent and material currently available suggests that the difficulties may be less than expected. For example, a unit on binary numbers, placed so as to develop the notion of place value, before a unit on decimals, would provide a helpful preliminary experience, but not an essential one. Thus, if some of the pupils do not complete the work on binary numbers they will not have omitted material that is essential to the course. On the other hand, pupils who are short of time for this work may well be those for whom the reinforcement it gives is most required; it is the least able children who most need repetition. It might be better to extend the faster pupils with some investigations – for example, ancillary work beyond the common core – thus avoiding the weakness found in many worksheets where able children simply do more complicated examples of work already mastered. It would also be important to remember, at later stages of the course, that there would be pupils who have omitted or not completed the work on binary numbers.

Similarly, a topic on tessellations following one on symmetry would pick up and use knowledge of line and half-turn symmetry, and symmetry of other orders, but a partial success in the earlier work would not make it impossible for the later work to be done. Again, a unit on some properties of plane figures, involving mid-points and parallels in a co-ordinate setting, following a previous unit on co-ordinates and the equations of lines, requires a basic knowledge of co-ordinates but does not actually use the knowledge of the equations of lines. In these last two examples, the omitted or uncompleted work can be covered at a later stage. The teacher must, however, be aware of the achievement of each pupil so that the necessary adjustment can be made at that time. The examples given are all from first- or second-stage material and clearly the problem becomes more acute at later stages of the course.

The implications of adopting mixed-ability grouping for the teaching of mathematics have been discussed in this chapter. Chapter IV attempts to identify and describe the different forms of such teaching by comparing teaching models. Factors which lead to good practice, solutions which seem to work in specific situations and a description of what was found to be successful (and why) are also presented.

IV. Some teaching models and current practices

During the working group's visits to schools, classes were observed and discussions held with teachers. From these investigations, some dominant teaching models became apparent. The model used depended on many factors, including the philosophy of the school and of the mathematics department, and the strengths and interests of the class teacher; the accommodation and resources were also important. Teachers did not necessarily confine themselves to one style of teaching; both with different classes and within classes varying styles were used. In general terms, it is felt that good mixed-ability teaching will involve the adoption of a variety of the three basic models described below.

TEACHING MODELS

Whole-class activity

This is characterized by all the pupils pursuing the same general theme at the same time. This may take the form of a topic, project or investigation. Within this activity pupils may be clearly differentiated, performing different tasks or exercises but all with the same general theme. Initially the whole class may be involved in the same task, but pupils become more clearly differentiated as they begin to explore these tasks at different levels. This differentiation can be catered for in several different ways. The most common way is by means of a topic booklet issued to the pupil at the beginning of the period of study; the teacher introduces the topic and the pupils then work through the booklet with help from the teacher. Further explanations to the whole class may be introduced during the course of study, depending on the degree of instruction in the booklet and the formality of the teacher.

A variation of this approach is a series of booklets on the same topic, graded in difficulty. The booklets produced by the Resources for Learning Development Unit, for example, have a star rating to indicate the degree of difficulty. The teacher assigns booklets to pupils according to their previous attainment.*

Another variation is a series of worksheets broken up into modules, each of

*For details of these and other widely used materials see Chapter VIII.

which is studied for a set period of time. Commercially published books used with this teaching model include *Resource Mathematics* and *Modular Mathematics*. Each module may contain a post-test, and sometimes a pre-test as in the Birmingham Structured Mathematics Scheme. A modular scheme which uses more sophisticated resources is the Hertfordshire Computer Managed Mathematics Project, where each module is introduced by a videotaped TV programme and worksheets are either teacher- or computer-marked.

Another form of whole-class activity involves exploratory tasks to which pupils respond by finding their own levels of investigation. The teacher is provided with notes or a package which may offer a description of the subject-matter, concept explanation, extensions, suggestions, activities for pupils and solutions. An example of this type of organization is provided in the South Nottinghamshire Project. The teacher introduces the problem to the whole class before setting the pupils to their task. Discussions between teacher and pupil, and between pupils, are essential ingredients of this approach. Whichever type of task is used, whether it is exercises designed to develop particular concepts, skills and techniques or exploratory tasks designed to develop the use of concepts by presenting them in unusual situations, the topic is usually studied for two or three weeks.

Group work

Groups of pupils are organized within the class to pursue different tasks. These groups may be formed through choice, randomly or by the teacher bringing together those pupils with the same interests. The group size may vary from two to eight pupils. Tasks, which may be either exercises or explorations, are provided from a wide variety of sources. They may take the form of school- or commercially produced topic booklets, work cards, or assignment sheets, or they may be textbooks. This teaching model relies very much on the teacher's familiarity with the material and his ability to maintain the different activities at the same time. He may assign tasks to groups according to ability and previous attainment, or the pupils may be given a choice. Small-group work obviously encourages discussions between pupils. During the lesson the teacher familiarizes himself with the work of each group by circulating and making sure that the decisions and activities of the group are not dominated by one member.

Individualized schemes

The most popular form of teaching model used with mixed-ability grouping is based on some sort of individualized scheme which aims to recognize and provide for distinct differences between pupils. The tasks are usually structured, although schemes do exist where a pupil is presented with a variety of work cards from which he chooses his own. Where pupil choice does exist a degree of teacher guidance is usually built in. The structured, individualized (some people prefer to call them personalized) schemes take several forms. Each pupil may proceed from one task to the next in linear fashion, his work being assessed as satisfactory by the teacher before he is allowed to proceed to the next task; the pupil may be tested after each task or during natural breaks in the scheme. The tasks may be assigned automatically from school-produced work cards, work-sheets or topic booklets, or a progress sheet may define a linear course by directing pupils to exercises in a textbook and providing homework and tests.

Another type of scheme, such as the SMP work cards, may involve a set of work cards organized into topics. Each topic contains a set of linearly sequenced work cards in sections, with preliminary cards for the less able and supplementary cards for the more able. At the end of each section the pupil completes a check card and test card before going on to the next section or topic, which is allotted by the teacher, assigned by a flowchart or chosen by the pupil.

In the Kent Mathematics Project and the Secondary Mathematics Individualized Learning Experiment a resource bank of materials is made available to the teacher. The teacher assigns about ten tasks (in the case of SMILE, or twelve, in the case of KMP) to the pupil in the form of what the project refers to as a matrix. The pupil completes the task in the matrix, marks it and then completes a test on each task. These tests are marked by the teacher, who defines a new matrix for the pupil according to the results of the tests and the flowchart topics available to him.

A variation of individualized schemes allows each pupil to be given the flowchart linking the tasks in the scheme. They organize their own work, choosing their own path on the flowchart, checking off the sections as completed and, if they wish, pursuing a topic beyond the main scheme through follow-up work. Pupils complete a weekly record for the teacher to check their progress.

The essential feature of an individualized scheme is a resource bank of material and tasks which may be in the form of work cards, worksheets or exercises from textbooks. Tasks may be assigned automatically by teacher recommendation, by pupil choice or a mixture of all three. In parts of the scheme for which individualized work cards are used, such as SMP cards or SMILE material, teachers have often restricted the range which is in use at any one time. This implies the possession of a larger number of sets of material than would be necessary otherwise, but if a scheme of alternating activities in successive fortnights is used, by staggering the different groups of classes within the year the material may be shared out more economically.

EXERCISES AND EXPLORATORY TASKS

The tasks used in whole-class activity, group work or individualized schemes may be either exercises or exploratory tasks. Exercises are usually short and are designed to develop particular concepts, skills or techniques. Exploratory tasks tend to be open-ended investigations designed to develop the use of concepts by presenting them in unusual situations; in this way previously learned concepts are reinforced, strategies such as classification, generalization and proof are developed, and the learning of new concepts is encouraged. Exploratory tasks seem far less popular with teachers, probably because of the initial difficulty of finding the kind of investigation which children can explore at their own ability level. There is also teachers' uncertainty in maintaining and supporting these open-ended activities in the classroom. Consequently, teachers tend to neglect the exploratory tasks in schemes which incorporate both types of material.

The reader will be familiar with tasks which take the form of exercises. These can be found in most schemes and in published texts such as the SMP *Main School Course* (lettered books) and the *Oxford Comprehensive Mathematics* series, both of which are used with mixed-ability classes.

Exploratory tasks in the form of investigations can be found in a variety of sources such as *Starting Points*, *Topics from Mathematics*, Leapfrogs *Network* material, Development of Ideas in Mathematical Education (DIME) Project's *Mathematics Workcard Booklets* and various pamphlets produced by the Association of Teachers of Mathematics (ATM). Two examples of investigations in use with mixed-ability classes are given below.

Example 1   Square cut

Start with a square. Now draw two straight lines, so that each line begins and ends on the perimeter of the square. For example:

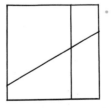

What shapes are formed by doing this?

Can you draw the lines so that the following shapes are made:

squares, rectangles, parallelograms, isosceles triangles, equilateral triangles, rhombuses?

What other shapes can you make?

How many different shapes is it possible to achieve in one go?

How many totally different situations are there?

Example 2   Bracelets

Start with any two numbers smaller than 10 (say 1 and 5).

Make a series of numbers like this: 1→ 5→ 6→ 1→ 7→ 8→ 5→ ?

Can you see how this series is obtained?

Write down the next six numbers in the series.

What happens to the series if you keep on going?

Choose some more starting numbers and investigate what happens.

How many different series can you make?

What happens if you use numbers in other bases?

THE RELATIONSHIP BETWEEN TEACHING MODELS, EXERCISES AND EXPLORATORY TASKS

Both exercises and exploratory tasks are used in the teaching models that emerged during the working group's school visits. These models and some of their distinguishing features are summarized in Table 1. A detailed comparison of the different teaching models follows and is illustrated by accounts of five of the lessons observed by members of the group.

Table 1 Various teaching models and some of their properties

Model	1. Exercises	2. Exploratory tasks
X Whole-class activity	All pupils study the same topic at the same time. Material is in the form of worksheets, work cards or topic work books.	Pupils are involved in various levels of investigation of a teacher-initiated problem or activity.
Y Group work	Small groups in the class work on different tasks from a text-book, topic book, worksheet or work card.	Small groups carry out different investigations or activities from a variety of sources.
Z Individualized schemes	Pupils work on materials from a structured scheme which is designed to develop concepts. The materials or tasks may be either sequenced linearly or in a flowchart. Task assignment is systematic or teacher directed.	The pupil works individually, choosing his tasks, with guidance from the teacher, from a bank of investigations, not necessarily structured.

A COMPARISON OF DIFFERENT TEACHING MODELS

Six characteristics were used to compare the various models described above. These were: organization in the classroom, tasks and their purpose, resources, the differentiation of tasks between different pupils, the teacher's role both inside and outside the classroom and discussions taking place in the classroom. The maintenance of continuity was a feature of the teacher's role in all models and is not repeated in the separate descriptions which follow.

Whole-class activity

Exercises (X.1)

Organization. The whole class is engaged on the same topic, project or theme; pupils may be working on different tasks within that topic. They work individually or in groups. The topic is usually decided by a departmental scheme or is chosen by the teacher.

Tasks. These are short exercises to develop skills, techniques, and concepts, or to provide calculations. The work involved could be a class project on a particular theme (for example, measurement, area).

Resources. Textbooks and published or teacher-produced worksheets, sometimes stapled together to provide topic booklets. Examples include SMP lettered books, *Oxford Comprehensive Mathematics,* the Oxford Mathematics Group's *Resource Mathematics.*

Differentiation. The less able pupils may only be able to complete the first part of the exercise successfully, while abler pupils will do more of the exercise set or go on to the harder exercises.

Teacher's role. Inside the classroom the teacher introduces topics at frequencies ranging from once every lesson to once per fortnight or three weeks. The teacher gives instruction, helps with individual difficulties and makes assessments. Outside the classroom his major activity is marking.

Discussions. Mainly teacher–pupil exchanges concerned with difficulties, assessment and progress.

Exploratory tasks (X.2)

Organization. Same as X.1.

Tasks. Mainly investigations which pupils explore at their own level.

Resources. Usually work cards. Teacher's notes explain the task, suggest extensions and offer suggestions for pupil activity. Examples include the South Nottinghamshire Project.

Differentiation. The less able pupils will only manage to spot the 'obvious' patterns and make simple deductions while the abler pupils will reach higher levels of abstraction, generalization, extension and explanation, and present more sophisticated write-ups.

Teacher's role. Inside the classroom he introduces investigations, suggests extensions, discusses progress and initiates discussion. Outside the classroom he organizes new material, examines extensions and marks work.

Discussions. Teacher–pupil exchanges include preliminary class discussion of the problem and procedures for investigation; on-going discussion during the activity about strategies, procedures and write-ups; discussion about results with individual pupils and the class, particularly at the end of a piece of work; decisions about new directions, including extending and generalizing results.

Group work

Exercises (Y.1)

Organization. Pupils in groups of from, say, two to eight. Different groups may be on different topics, either by choice or teacher direction.

Tasks. Short exercises or activities to develop skills and techniques or to provide calculations.

Resources. A variety of work cards, textbooks or short topic booklets are made available. The materials contain some instruction and explanation.

Differentiation. Tasks are assigned to groups according to ability, previous attainment, interests or choice.

Teacher's role. Inside the classroom he supervises various groups; introduces topics to them; interprets booklets; helps with difficulties; assesses work; discusses progress with separate groups; provides extensions and new work at the appropriate time; and makes sure that no group is dominated by one individual. Outside the classroom he marks work and monitors the progress of individuals within a group.

Discussions. Exchanges between pupils are concerned with starting a task, discussing solutions and comparing progress. Teacher–pupil exchanges include questioning individual pupils on their work, assessing it, suggesting new work, helping with difficulties, offering encouragement.

Exploratory tasks (Y.2)

Characteristics are the same as in Y.1 except for:

Tasks. These are mainly investigations or activities which pupils explore together within the group.

Resources. Assignment cards or booklets. Examples include Leapfrogs booklets; *Topics from Mathematics*; DIME booklets.

Individualized schemes

Exercises (Z.1)

Organization. Each pupil has his own personal task. Several pupils could be doing the same task but they do not usually work together. Pupils proceed to the next item or task according to a scheme or to teacher direction.

Tasks. Instructions and an explanation followed by short exercises to develop skills and concepts.

Resources. A bank of either school- or commercially produced work cards organized in a flowchart, sequentially ordered worksheets, topic booklets, or textbooks. Materials are made available in a filing cabinet, stack or wall-rack. Preliminary or supplementary cards may be integrated into the scheme. Examples include KMP, SMILE and SMP work cards and textbooks.

Differentiation. All pupils proceed at their own pace doing different cards according to ability. It does not necessarily follow that the more able do more cards, because these vary in difficulty. Systematic task assignment or assignment by the teacher according to previous attainment and performance (for example, as recorded in the form of a matrix).

Teacher's role. Inside the classroom he is a manager who assigns tasks, helps pupils to choose tasks and to follow a scheme, and helps with individual difficulties. Outside the classroom he maintains the system, marks work, diagnoses difficulties, decides on the length of time a pupil should be spending on a card, and devises new tasks to complement or supplement the system.

Discussions. Teacher—pupil exchanges concern the discussion of work, assessment, help with difficulties, organizational problems and the assignment of new tasks. Exchanges between pupils are necessarily fewer than for other types of model but those which do occur concern the checking of solutions.

Exploratory tasks (Z.2)

The same as Z.1 except for:

Tasks. Investigations and applications of different skills, techniques and concepts.

CLASSROOM PRACTICE

In this section descriptions of lessons observed are given to illustrate the different kinds of models which are used in mixed-ability mathematics classes. (The time allocations given are, of course, approximations.)

Class A

(Whole-class exercises; length of lesson: 70 minutes; class size: 56)

Two fourth-year classes were put together with two teachers. A teaching area large enough for the fifty-six pupils was created by pushing back a screen which separated two classrooms. Some tables were pushed together and some left as units; the children then worked mostly in pairs, though some worked singly and some in larger groups of up to six children.

All the pupils were studying mensuration, which formed part of a fortnightly cycle of different topics. At the beginning of the lesson the pupils collected their topic booklet from a central point. These booklets had been prepared by the mathematics staff at the school and consisted of worksheets stapled together. No instruction was given to the class; the instructions on the sheet were considered by the teachers to provide sufficient explanation. On most of the sheets the explanation consisted of the statement of a formula, a worked example and some calculations to be done by the pupils. The class was involved in a wide variety of tasks from the linear set of worksheets containing exercises on the following topics:

1 The area of a rectangle. The area of a triangle.
2 The area of a parallelogram. The area of a trapezium.
3 The area of a circle. Miscellaneous problems.
4 Problems on Worksheets 1 and 2. Further circle problems.
5 Volume of a cuboid. Volume of a prism.
6 Volume of a pyramid. Volume of a cone.
7 Volume of a sphere. Surface area of a sphere.
8 Miscellaneous problems.

At the end of the two-week session, during which the abler pupils had completed more of the booklet than the less able, the teachers assessed the work in the loose-leaf file presented by each pupil and recorded a mark out of ten. They provided the pupil with a written comment on his work on the booklet and on a post-test which was completed at the end of a topic. A structured homework sheet given at the start of the topic was also marked by the teacher.

Movement round the class was restricted by the teachers, whose roles during the lesson were to maintain the informal atmosphere of the class and guide the pupils through the worksheets as quickly and efficiently as possible. They spent their time:

	per cent
dealing with three restless pupils	5
organizing worksheets and providing equipment	10
helping with difficulties and interpreting questions	45
encouraging pupils and praising task completion	20
carrying out informal assessment	20.

The role of the teachers in the classroom tended to restrict teacher–pupil discussion to exchanges about difficulties and progress. Although there were a few isolates in the class, most pupils worked together in pairs enthusiastically and with a spirit of self-help. During the lesson observed, it appeared that when pupils worked in pairs no one pupil dominated the other and that pupils of similar ability tended to work together. Discussions between pupils were encouraged and were mainly concerned with difficulties and the checking of solutions.

Class B

(Whole-class and group explorations; length of lesson: 60 minutes; class size 29)

At the beginning of this first-year lesson the teacher introduced the activity to the class, who were mainly working in pairs. The activity, taken from published material, was an investigation of lattice paths with a view to establishing the concept of shortest route. Pupils were provided with square lattices on paper and given a series of questions leading them to explore the ways in which routes between points could be mapped. The questions became more generalized with more options as the pupils worked through them. The school had produced overhead projector transparencies and teacher's notes to accompany the published material, indicating the concepts and strategies that could be developed and suggesting further work for the most able pupils, such as Pascal's Triangle and triangular lattices.

During the discussion about shortest routes the teacher drew the children's attention to various aspects of the problem and made it clear that they must record the shortest route for each dot in turn, marking it on 'dotty' paper with a felt pen. She then went round the class asking questions, checking solutions, giving advice, clarifying the activity, discussing strategy, making individual contributions available to the whole class, and generally keeping the children on the right track. The children made heavy demands on her and she was constantly on the move. She spent her time:

	per cent
introducing the activity	10
discussing strategies and helping	25
checking solutions	25
discussing solutions	25
suggesting extensions	15.

The pupils found the investigation interesting and appeared well motivated. Discussion was an essential ingredient of the lesson and pupils were encouraged to compare results and talk about their write-ups.

Class C

(Group exercises; lesson length: 70 minutes; class size: 22)

The teacher had already marked the pupils' books before this first-year lesson began. This assessment was very important as it enabled him to diagnose difficulties and ensure that each individual's mathematical development was maintained, not least by helping him make a decision about what a pupil could do next. If a pupil produced a piece of work which was, for them, particularly good it was immediately made into a wall display. Tasks were assigned to groups according to previous attainment and current needs. The topics chosen related to a general scheme of themes for the first and second years, but the approach was flexible.

On entering the room the children helped themselves to the books, textbooks and equipment which had carefully been laid out at the side of the room by the teacher before the lesson began. Most children wanted to work in pairs and the majority settled down to work with their partners; others preferred to work on their own. The teacher organized those who needed help with equipment before attending to those who needed new work.

One boy was going to the coast during the next week: what was the best route? A large-scale road map was produced and the teacher began to question the pupil.

'What do you mean by "best"?'
'Is there more than one way of getting there?'
'Which is the shortest route?'
'Will it be the quickest?'
'Why?'
'How long will it take?'
'How much petrol will we need?'
'What will it cost?'

Once the boy had been helped to organize his task, the teacher gathered around himself a group of eight pupils to whom he talked about finding powers from tables, asking them many questions.

'What does 22^2 mean?'
'How would you find it?'
'Is there a quicker way than multiplication?'
'Use tables. Correct! How?'
'What about 2.2^2?'
'Try these!'

These pupils were given examples to do. Various activities were taking place in the classroom, with the children involved in the following topics:

Powers and roots
Work set by the teacher, squaring numbers. Some pupils finding square roots. Eight pupils.

Areas of borders

Finding areas of flower-beds etc. Working from H. A. Shaw and F. E. Wright, *Discovering Mathematics*, Book 1 (Edward Arnold, metric edn, 1975). Five pupils.

The tetrahedron

Construction using nets. Working from Stuart E. Bell, *Mathematics in the Making*, Book 3: Looking at Solids (Longmans, 1970). Three pupils.

The circle

Calculations checked by cutting out the circle and measuring circumference with cotton. G. Marshall, *A World of Mathematics*, Book 5 (Nelson, 1972). Five pupils.

Routes

One boy planned his route to Scarborough from a road map. He completed the project on various aspects of the journey (for example, mileage, fuel required, cost per mile).

The teacher knew the pupils very well and spent his time going round the class questioning, extending and encouraging. The discussion was not limited to those who were stuck but centred round what pupils were doing and getting them to use the language of mathematics. The teacher made an attempt to talk to every pupil in the class and to mark as much work as possible. He spent his time in the following way:

administration, organization, providing new work   50 per cent

talking, questioning, working with children   50 per cent.

Class D

(Group exploratory tasks; lesson length: 60 minutes; class size: 27)

Before the workshop began the teacher had laid out on a side bench some Leapfrogs *Network* booklets, some DIME *Mathematics Workcard Booklets* and relevant materials (see Fig. 2). The booklets were designed to encourage the pupils to use mathematics in unusual situations, to provide opportunities to apply already familiar concepts or to provide experiences which might be needed

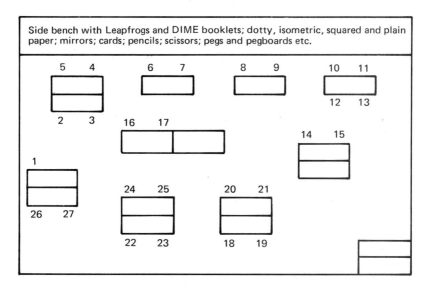

Fig. 2 Seating arrangement and materials for Class D workshop

in the future. Within these terms of reference pupils were free to organize both their materials and tasks.

On entering the room the pupils selected their own activity from the booklets and began to settle down. The teacher encouraged them to work in pairs since he felt that this provided more stimulus, more ideas and more fruitful discussion. However, several pupils decided to work on their own. During the lesson the teacher spent the whole time circulating, helping, discussing and suggesting. The activities in which the pupils were involved are shown in Table 2.

With ten minutes of the hour-long lesson remaining the equipment and materials were put away and all pupils were issued with their own little notebook. For the last five minutes of the lesson the children recorded a brief personal description of the activity they had been involved in during the lesson. It should be emphasized that the pupils took a lot of responsibility for the continuity of their work; to find the point of re-entry to their tasks they were able to refer to an experiment notebook in which they had recorded their previous work and tasks. Their own note-taking was essential to both the workshop activity and to maintaining continuity.

Table 2 Activities and materials in Class D workshop

Pupil	Activity	Source	Equipment
1	Making and sketching solids made with cubes	DIME Workcard Booklet, *Sketching Solids* (3D Sketching series)	Cubes, isometric dotty paper
2 and 3	Making up rules for mazes	Leapfrogs booklet *Leads* (pp. 52–3)	Squared paper
4 and 5	Investigating different arrangements of four cubes	Leapfrogs booklet *Cubes* (p. 12)	Interlock cubes, graph paper
6	Investigating parcels of different sizes	Leapfrogs booklet *Cubes* (p. 4)	Interlock cubes, string
7	Cups and downs: arrangement of three cups, symbolization using C and D	Leapfrogs booklet *Moves* (p. 7)	Cups
8 and 9	Sketching moves made in three dimensions	DIME Workcard Booklet, *Turning and Toppling*, (3D Sketching series)	Cubes, mirrors, isometric dotty paper
10 11 and 12	Cuboids: number of cubes in different box shapes	Leapfrogs booklet *Cubes* (p. 3)	Interlock cubes
13	Animals: making patterns with five counters	Leapfrogs booklet *Moves* (p. 12)	Counters
14 and 15 16 and 17	Count-a-counter puzzle: finding the least number of moves to invert a triangle made with counters	Leapfrogs booklet *Moves* (p. 1)	Counters
18 19 and 20	Next to: investigating arrangements of pegs on a 3 x 3 pegboard using a rule	Leapfrogs booklet *Pegboards* (p. 4)	Pegs, pegboards
21	Investigating single-layer solids	DIME Workcard Booklet *Sketching Solids*, (3D Sketching series)	Interlock cubes, isometric dotty paper

Table 2 — cont'd

Pupil	Activity	Source	Equipment
22 and 23	Patterns: investigation of how many different patterns can be made on a	Leapfrogs booklet *Pegboards* (p. 1)	Pegs, pegboard, square dotty paper
24 and 25	3 x 3 board using three pegs, two pegs and one peg		
26 and 27	Making optical illusions	Leapfrogs booklet *Leads* (p. 17)	Coloured card, scissors

Class E

(Individualized exercises; lesson length: 35 minutes; class size: 22)

The tables were arranged in rows facing the front, where the teacher's desk, filing cabinet and cupboard containing equipment were situated. At the beginning of the lesson a pupil issued folders containing exercise books and progress sheets to his colleagues. The pupils found the relevant SMP lettered book and started work. Some of them used the SMP teacher's guides to mark previous work.

The essential component of this highly structured scheme was the progress sheet which guided the pupil through both the SMP lettered books and supplementary work from other sources. This was achieved by dividing the course up into topics, defining exercises to be done, and showing which homework sheets were to be completed at any particular stage of the course. When a pupil had completed an exercise he marked it, using the answers in the teacher's guide, and corrected his work if necessary. If there was an aspect of the work that he did not understand he consulted the teacher. When an exercise had been completed the pupil crossed it off his sheet and proceeded to the next one.

This school was interesting in that an extra room was timetabled and staffed for testing. Tests were built into the course at regular stages and when a pupil reached a recommended test in his progress sheet he consulted a timetable on the wall which told him in which classroom the testing was taking place during that lesson. When a child had completed a test the teacher marked it and returned it during the next lesson. If a child did not achieve at least half marks he had to repeat the test after revision supervised by the teacher. The tests were diagnostic, attempting to test all the concepts and skills covered since the previous one. The teacher used the test to monitor progress, isolate problem areas and help the pupil.

The pupils worked on their own on a variety of topics from the SMP lettered books including:

prime numbers
tessellations
equivalent fractions
mappings
ordered pairs
binary arithmetic
combining shifts on a number line
multiplying fractions
percentages.

With this highly individualized scheme there was little conversation between the pupils. Teacher—pupil discussions were concerned with administrative problems and difficulties with tasks. During the lesson the teacher did no formal assessment and spent her time in the following way:

at her desk	per cent
guiding children through, and administration of, progress sheets	10
giving advice to children who asked for help on the exercise and mark sheets	50
moving round the class	
giving help to weaker children who did not ask for assistance	10
discussing, encouraging and ensuring productive output	30.

SUMMARY

Descriptions have been given of three basic teaching models found in schools visited by the working group. Some schools seemed to be unaware that teaching in mixed-ability groups could be accomplished in any way other than the one which had been developed within their own local situation. Again, some seemed to have developed an emphasis in work allocation on the performance of exercises, almost to the exclusion of exploratory investigations. With resources

48

there tended similarly to be an over-reliance on one type of material as against another (for example, school-produced worksheets to the exclusion of commercially produced materials and textbooks). That there is a wide variety of approach possible and a wide choice of materials available should now be clear. Reference will be made to these points in Chapter V, where we consider our findings and recommendations.

V. Results of the inquiry and recommendations

This chapter summarizes the findings of the working group and closes with their major recommendations. It is important to remember that the comments below are summaries and will not be fully understood without a careful reading of the earlier chapters of the report, which give arguments and examples at greater length. The case studies in Chapter VII will also illuminate the statements made here.

The sample of schools on which these results are based was neither large nor randomly selected. Schools were suggested by local education authorities and by members of the working group, with the expectation that their methods and their solutions to the various problems of teaching mixed-ability classes might be of interest and help to other schools. Twenty-six schools were visited, by two members of the group wherever possible. Nineteen of the schools were either 11−16 or 11−18, five were 13−18, one was 9−13 and one 11−14. Mixed-ability teaching was the school policy in all schools visited.

FINDINGS

Advantages and disadvantages

This question was discussed in general terms in Chapter I. In the survey we found that teachers felt they had gained the following advantages from the adoption of mixed-ability grouping:

    i   Social benefits.

    ii   Curriculum development: they had to re-think aims and objectives and introduce new ideas into the classroom.

    iii   Team-work: it had forced them to work together. The resultant team-work and a consistent approach had made it easier to integrate new members of staff.

    iv   Teachers were more aware of individual differences between pupils and the need to cater for these differences.

v   A good working atmosphere was created in the classroom, there were fewer behaviour problems and closer contact was established between teacher and pupil.

vi   It raised the levels of expectation of both teachers and pupils; pupils lost the sense of defeat or failure sometimes experienced in mathematics and gained a sense of enjoyment and achievement.

vii   There was more variety for the teacher in the class.

The disadvantages which the teachers felt persisted included the following:

i   The difficulty of providing for the less able and very able, in terms of finding suitable work.

ii   The difficulty of providing and organizing a variety of materials in the classroom.

iii   Problems associated with continuity: how to introduce a topic for the second time.

iv   The problem of finding an efficient allocation of the teacher's time in the classroom.

v   The resulting heavy demands made on the teacher both inside and outside the classroom.

vi   The exclusion of the teacher from effective interaction with pupils in some schemes.

Departmental preparation and the role of the head of department

The inquiry revealed that when mixed-ability grouping is adopted by a department it requires a concerted effort on the part of all members of the department if it is to be achieved successfully. It is unwise to take such a step without a reasonably united and enthusiastic team. The head of department must expect to provide a considerable measure of support, guidance and advice to his members of staff as they attempt to learn new techniques and to adopt new roles. At the same time the need for team-work and co-operation can lead to personal development on the part of the teachers involved.

It was found that before introducing mixed-ability teaching it is important to have sufficient discussion of the mathematical aims and objectives for the various classes of pupil at different stages of the course. Teachers found it necessary to experiment, to evaluate the success of the methods adopted and to be prepared to abandon those which were not successful. Some schools have begun by introducing mixed ability into half of the first year, rather than the whole year, and have evaluated the achievements of pupils in the two types of grouping at the end of the year. (In the two cases of this which we have met, the teachers in the departments reported that they found no substantial differences in levels of achievement, either at the extremes or in the middle of the ability range.) This partial introduction allowed the necessary experiments in organization to be made on a smaller scale and mistakes, if any, to be rectified before too many pupils were involved.

It may appear from the foregoing that only the exceptional teacher can be expected to make a success of mixed-ability teaching. However, in the departments we have seen there was plenty of evidence that, given good departmental organization and a supportive head of department, many teachers who would be modest about their individual capacities have tackled the new problems with success.

Teaching models

Of the twenty-six schools visited, twelve made exclusive use of some form of whole-class teaching, none relied totally on group work, seven used an individualized scheme, and seven used a variety of methods. More schools were using whole-class activity than were using a totally individualized scheme, but seven of these schools taught by means of linearly sequenced worksheets.

Whatever methods they used teachers emphasized their concern for the continuity of the learning of pupils, but it was clear that this had at least two different interpretations. Sometimes it referred to continuity of experience for the class as a whole and at other times to continuity of experience for the individual pupil. The development of pupil autonomy and opportunities for them to organize their own learning was not particularly evident. In individualized schemes a large proportion of the teaching time appeared to be taken up in administration. Discussion among pupils and between teacher and pupils occurred rarely in the individualized classes. It was more apparent where whole-class methods were used and particularly in some of the latter where exploratory tasks were an important feature of the work.

The majority of schools visited employed only one teaching model for all their work. This restriction was sometimes a result of teachers' unfamiliarity with other methods of working and sometimes arose from a conviction that they had found the 'ideal solution'. The working group were agreed that the seven schools which used a variety of teaching models were the most successful schools visited. All but one of these incorporated an individualized work card component and all but two also used some group work. More forms of genuine pupil choice were evident and the teachers appeared to be more than usually sympathetic to the needs of the pupils. A school successful at offering variety organized fortnightly programmes of three kinds of work:

a the development of number skills and understanding using SMP cards;

b workshop activities, during which the pupils had free choice from a range of tasks of an exploratory type (the set of tasks available to a particular class was varied from one half term to the next);

c teacher-introduced whole-class activities — these might most appropriately be applications (for example, statistical surveys).

In these activities it was possible for groups of pupils of differing ability to work together.

Materials

Ten schools used their own material as the basis of their work, six used some form of locally produced material, three used SMP cards, four used a textbook and three used a variety of sources including their own material. However, this categorization was by no means clear cut since many schools supplemented their basic provision by additional material either of their own or from elsewhere. The use of a variety of materials did seem to be an important factor in a successful scheme.

School-produced material. This took two distinct forms:

a self-contained worksheets or work cards designed to replace or supplement commercial material;

b director sheets, often with a few introductory remarks and examples, which directed the pupil to other resources.

Schools which relied entirely on their own school-produced material were generally less successful than those using material produced commercially or by a consortium. The mathematical diet offered was often thin, restricting pupils' activity to using skills in a limited way. Problems and exploratory tasks were rarely incorporated.

It also appeared that teachers were often more inhibited by using internally produced material than they were by using material obtained from elsewhere, so much so that in some cases the material appeared to form a barrier between teacher and pupils. The co-operative production of material for teaching within school offers a valuable educational experience for teachers in terms of curriculum development and departmental interaction. However, the considerable commitment of time and energy which it requires did not always appear to be well used. Often teachers were too busy in writing new material for later years to improve and extend that first written, or to provide tasks at various levels. Thus material continued to be used even though it had proved unsuitable for many children. The claim that an advantage of school-produced material is that it can be discarded if found unsuitable was not substantiated in practice. In fact only one school had abandoned a scheme relying entirely on their own material: they had adopted a commercial scheme with their own supplements.

The production of material directing pupils to a variety of sources would seem to be a more profitable use of staff time. In the schools visited, such material was often successful and allowed teachers and pupils to use tasks from a wide variety of sources including their own work cards, worksheets and problem suggestions.

Material produced by local consortia. Material produced by a local collaborative activity had a number of merits. Both the mathematical content and the standard of presentation were generally superior to those of school-produced material. These were the result of the more extensive feedback and evaluation obtained and the availability of better facilities for reproduction. Teachers remarked on the benefits of pooling ideas, experiences and expertise, and the fact that their writing skills improved.

Published schemes. The exclusive adoption of a ready-made scheme created problems. It made it difficult to incorporate material from other sources and difficult for the teachers to inject any of their own thinking into it. Successful schools used published schemes as a framework, supplementing them with material of their own.

The age range for mixed-ability teaching

In those schools which received children at 11, nearly half adopted grouping based on attainment after the second year. Few of these schools would go back to grouping by ability in the first two years; the level of expectation of both pupils and teachers had risen. There were some departments which had continued mixed-ability grouping into later years but had subsequently reverted to setting after the second year. This was for various reasons, such as the lack of suitable teaching material, the increasing spread in attainment or the departure of teachers who had pioneered and organized the scheme. No school we visited had gone back to setting in the first year. There appeared to be no general relationship between the quality of the work throughout the school and the point at which mixed-ability classes were reorganized into sets. Some schools had established successful first-year work and in the view of visiting members of the working group would have been quite capable of continuing mixed-ability groups into the second year, but did not intend to do so. Of those schools which continued mixed-ability teaching up to the fourth year or beyond, some appeared to be operating successfully while others, in our view, would have better served their pupils by grouping them by attainment much earlier than they were doing. In some cases the persistence of the mixed-ability work in mathematics was due to the ethos of the school rather than to the particular competence of the mathematics department.

Such schools as successfully took mixed-ability teaching beyond the third year had Mode III provision for many subjects in CSE and in one case for GCE O level as well. There was a substantial amount of course-work assessment in mathematics in these schools. One school did not enter pupils for O level, all external examinations being Mode III CSE. Double entry was used at two schools.

At the point in the school at which mixed-ability grouping was stopped, parallel setting was the most usual form of re-grouping. Sets were formed within sections of the year, each section consisting of either half or a third of the year. No school formed sets across the whole year group, though there was one school in which streaming across the whole year group was adopted. On the other hand, there were schools in which an even broader form of setting was used: the more able were extracted for an O-level course, and in some of these schools the least able were also removed. The remainder of the year group stayed in mixed-ability classes. This practice is popularly called 'topping and tailing'.

Of the five schools taking children at 13, three taught mixed-ability groups for the first year only, mainly as a diagnostic device, following this by setting in two cases and by topping and tailing in another. One school continued mixed ability into the second year and one into the third.

Choice – for pupils and teachers

Self-discipline and co-operation are important aspects of mixed-ability teaching. Children were not always encouraged to develop these qualities because they were not given the opportunity to organize their own learning by choosing their own tasks. Pupil choice was encountered in only three schools, where it took the following forms:

i a pupil chose a task from the variety provided (for example, Leapfrogs booklets; work cards) or agreed on a 'contract' with the teacher;

55

ii a pupil was allowed to extend a topic he was interested in (this relied on the teacher's confidence and skill).

In both of these provisions there had to be an acceptance by the teacher that different pupils may reach the same end-point by different routes. Although little provided for, choice has these advantages:

i it creates a sense of involvement and motivation;

ii the pupil has a good chance of presenting himself with the right level of challenge; this, together with thoughtful teacher intervention, can ensure that the pupil is tackling suitable tasks.

In any system of choice there is a need for involvement by the teacher to set up the situation and make it work. Teacher choice is crucial in this process. The following conditions need to be satisfied:

i the teacher must choose and devise tasks which will achieve the aims of the scheme and the philosophy behind it;

ii the teacher must be aware of the content of the tasks he has presented to the children;

iii the teacher must have the skill to allow the pupils to develop and use their experience of the range of material available; he must make them aware of what is available before they can make an initial choice;

iv the teacher must guide the pupil by offering a structured set of tasks, rather than a rag-bag of isolated activities, and by knowing when and where to intervene, to offer advice and make follow-up suggestions. The importance of discussion in this process cannot be overstated.

Diagnosis and treatment

Teachers recognized that for successful mixed-ability teaching in mathematics there should be:

i continuity and development of mathematical ideas;

ii diagnosis of difficulties followed by appropriate action.

To achieve these, the teacher had to be aware of the structure of mathematics and the structure and aims of his course, as well as being familiar with his materials. He also needed access to suitable tasks which would develop skills, concepts, relationships and strategies.

Assessment and the recording of pupils' progress

Assessment has three main purposes:

i to provide both the pupil and the teacher with a measure of the pupil's achievement;

ii to identify weaknesses and difficulties and to enable decisions about the pupil's future work to be made;

iii to enable the teacher to gauge the general effectiveness of his own teaching.

The first of these include:

a the continuing dialogue between teacher and pupil, in which the teacher will mix encouragement with a critical evaluation of the pupil's work;

b an objective measure of the pupil's level of attainment in relation to the syllabus and the class as a whole. The teacher will need to record the topic or tasks covered by the pupil with a general note on his level of success with them.

There is considerable confusion about these different aspects of assessment, particularly in systems requiring a single overall grade to be recorded for a pupil.

The means of securing interaction between teacher and pupil by marking and discussion of the pupil's work is not greatly different in a mixed-ability class from a setted one. It is worth noting that in those individualized schemes where periodic tests are provided, it is important for the teacher to intervene at that point to ensure that the pupil has understood what has been done. It may be necessary to get the pupil to repeat a sequence or to do supplementary work, which will also need to be assessed and recorded.

Various types of formal assessment exist. A pupil may complete tests on a set of work cards. These are marked by the teacher, who uses the results to define the pupil's next set of tasks; to overcome difficulties this may include work on the same level as before. SMILE uses this system. In the Hertfordshire Computer

Managed Mathematics Project the pupil's work is marked by either the teacher or a computer; if he gets a particular example wrong he is told to complete a similar example on a sheet containing extra or remedial questions. There are also teacher-designed schemes with built-in tests.

One way of keeping records of individualized work is to construct a class matrix where either pupil or teacher ticks off the tasks as completed. This may be supplemented by the pupil himself keeping a record of tasks performed. It is important for the department to have some well-organized system for such record-keeping which does not take an undue amount of the teacher's time and energy away from actual teaching. The teacher who has frequent conversations with pupils will know far better what their attainment is than one who has only ensured that the requisite number of ticks have been made on the matrix.

When the assessment of course-work is needed for examinations it is necessary to ensure that all the teachers in the department are awarding grades at the same level. Some CSE boards and some schools have produced structured schemes which give a number of headings under which a grade must be given. These are helpful in ensuring a higher level of agreement and objectivity.

Coherence and structure

Although ostensibly structuring their work, some schools presented mathematics as just a bundle of facts and skills and not a way of working, a way of thinking, a variety of processes requiring their correct selection and application to unfamiliar problems and situations.

Because of the structure of many well-intentioned schemes some teachers and pupils become 'locked in'. Such schemes may be allowed to dominate the teaching to such an extent that teachers find it impossible to substitute their own material or develop pupils' interests. Mixed-ability approaches should provide coherence and continuity for classes but at the same time allow the teacher to introduce his own material in order to meet current demands, to provoke ideas and motivate pupils. Any system should allow for a teacher to pursue his and the pupils' interests. The experience of writing material can be a valuable one but, as we have already described, it can have disadvantages if carried too far. There must always be a place for teachers to inject their own ideas into their teaching.

Discussion

Many classrooms were characterized by their lack of discussion; in fact it is positively discouraged in some. In good mixed-ability lessons with a variety of approaches, exchanges between pupils and between teacher and pupil regularly take place. Teacher intervention is essential in individualized schemes where the pupil has little chance to discuss his work with his colleagues. Evidence gathered by the working group confirms the statement in a recent HMI report:[32] 'Schemes of individualized learning can give a low status to language and to learning by the spoken word.' It is also important in group and class work if discussion between pupils is to be initiated. Discussion needs to be developed in the following areas:

i At present, discussion between pupils is rarely seen as a way of deciding strategies, helping to solve problems, and so on. This is probably due to most teachers' inexperience in managing this kind of discussion and to a lack of suitable assignment material.

ii Teacher—pupil discussion is often one-sided, seen only in terms of help, instruction, assessment and explanation, and not in terms of encouraging responses from the pupil. The teacher needs to establish a relaxed classroom atmosphere so that he has time to think on the job, has time to listen to what the pupils are saying (the best method of assessment) and to talk *with* the pupils.

iii Discussion between teachers is essential if they are to put their own experiences into a framework of their colleagues' experience.

a   There is a need to develop a non-authoritarian and co-operative atmosphere, with frequent and open exchanges about methods, successes and failures (and how the last can be rectified).

b   Consistency of mathematical education is a major problem for many heads of department. It could be helped by discussion and team teaching.

c   There is surprisingly little discussion with feeder schools. This could play a great part in easing the transfer of pupils and maintaining continuity in the mathematical learning of individual pupils.

d   Relationships between departments within the school were often only on the 'nodding acquaintance' level. The application of mathematical techniques in other subjects in the school was rarely discussed and departments seemed unaware of the content of the courses or requirements of other departments.

The basic choice involved here is whether the pupils at the extremes of the ability range are provided with special tasks in the classroom or are withdrawn. Withdrawal can be for a year or longer to provide for those with basic difficulties or for a few weeks to help some pupils overcome particular weaknesses before they return to their usual classes. Among the schools visited, nearly half extracted non-readers, pupils with extreme difficulties in basic number, or disturbed pupils, by placing them in special groups with separate courses and specialist remedial teachers.

No schools visited provided for the most able pupils by withdrawal during the first two years. A few schools had separate classes for potential O-level candidates in the fourth and fifth years.

Just over half the schools visited tried to provide for the whole ability range in the same classroom. Not all of these schools succeeded in providing for the most and least able in these classes. In those schools using a linear scheme with little or no supplementary work all pupils worked through a series of common tasks and differentiation between pupils related only to the speed at which they worked. The bright pupils were under-stretched and the less able were not always provided with suitable tasks or support. However, it was rare to come across the totally demoralized 'bottom-streamer' in any mixed-ability class.

Pupils of different ability were most successfully provided for in those schools where a variety of resources were in use. Sometimes the teacher directed individual pupils to different books or cards or had prepared a number of different assignments on the same topic from which he could choose tasks to give to a particular pupil; some of the locally produced collaborative schemes provide these different assignments. In SMILE and the Kent Mathematics Project the teacher can guide the pupil through a series of easier or more difficult tasks as required. The South Nottinghamshire Project provides tasks which each contain extensions which may be offered to the more able pupils and may involve a variation on the original situation, a generalization from it, or perhaps provoke a more determined effort to explain why a particular generalization is true.

'Float' teachers. Six schools visited used a system of bringing in additional help for the whole or part of the year group for all or part of the time. Sometimes four teachers were allocated to three classes and sometimes teachers gave up non-teaching periods to allow the continuance of a system which they saw being successful; sometimes sixth-form pupils came in to help.

The role of floaters varied from school to school but included the following: helping the less able or extending the more able, providing supplementary material, preparing material, helping with general organization and helping young teachers. In one school two floaters operated in a year group of six classes: one found which pupils had difficulties by scrutinizing the assessment records, class work and test marks; the other, a remedial specialist, diagnosed the difficulties and gave help to pupils either in the classroom or in small groups withdrawn from it. In another school a float teacher was responsible for administering tests built into the individualized linear course.

Homework

Not all schools visited felt that it was essential always to set homework, at least during the first two years. However, other schools attached sufficient weight to homework to overcome the difficulties that admittedly arose for mixed-ability classes. One obvious difficulty is whether work cards may be taken home: in some schools a 'signing out' scheme is used to encourage pupils to continue work begun in class, and for set homework. Another possibility is to provide for homework supplementary worksheets linked to the class worksheets; otherwise pupils may have to be given work to do at home that is unrelated to what they are doing in class, and this will break the continuity. Pupils who are involved with exploratory tasks or investigations can write up the results for homework.

Content

Mixed-ability teaching in mathematics is often associated with what is often called, for want of a better word, 'modern' mathematics. In practice many schools are finding many 'traditional' topics very suitable for this mode of teaching; mixed-ability classes in mathematics were encountered in schools whose total syllabus could be regarded as traditional in nature.

Accommodation and facilities

Whether or not mixed-ability teaching requires special accommodation depends on the extent to which new teaching methods are to be adopted. An individual worksheet or work card system clearly requires nothing beyond the traditional rows of desks, whereas if group work is to be attempted a more flexible arrangement will be required. Generally it is necessary to provide for somewhat more movement in the classroom; larger rooms have helped with this. For systems such as SMILE or individualized workcards there needs to be storage for those materials to which the pupils have access. Similarly, if methods involving practical materials and apparatus are to be employed a central store and adjacent mathematics rooms are a great advantage. If a float teacher is available the classrooms which he is serving will need to be close to each other. It can also be very helpful to have some small space close by to which small groups can be withdrawn.

A large variety of equipment was found to be preferable but not essential. What is certainly needed are the resources to produce material as required, adequate storage space and a retrieval system which enables a variety of materials to be readily available and easily accessible. Access to a spirit duplicating machine was found to be almost essential.

The timetabling of several classes at a single time (blocking) is also helpful but not essential. It is also helpful to have lessons of about an hour since the organizational problems at the beginning and end of a lesson mean that longer lessons tend to be more efficient. These longer periods of study aid differentiation and continuity since the pupils have more time to get on with further work; the teacher also has more time to become aware of the activities in the class.

During the survey successful mixed-ability teaching was seen to operate in classes of up to thirty-three pupils per teacher.

Evaluation

As with every other aspect of education the question of evaluation in relation to mixed-ability teaching is of vital importance. While we found schools which appeared to give only scant attention to this matter there were others which constantly kept under review their methods, materials and teaching models. Where mixed-ability groups were confined to the first year or two many teachers considered the question of evaluation largely in terms of the pupils' interest, enjoyment and personal development. Those few schools which carried mixed-ability classes on into the fifth form were able to evaluate their methods, to some extent at any rate, in relation to their pupils' success or otherwise in external examinations. The working group would like to see teachers paying more attention to evaluation independently of the pressure of external examinations.

RECOMMENDATIONS

1. Planning

When embarking on mixed-ability teaching the department will need to meet to plan in advance the steps of the enterprise and to agree the policy in relation to different aspects of the work. The planning will need to be concerned not merely with administration and organization but also with the general philosophy of the department in relation to mixed-ability teaching.

2. Pace of introduction

If introducing mixed-ability teaching, tackle one year at a time. Only move on to attempt the second year once the department is satisfied that suitable differentiation of tasks and sufficient continuity has been achieved for all the different pupils. Schools which tried to introduce two years at a time found it a difficult and exhausting proposition. Some departments may prefer to start with half a year rather than a whole year and compare results.

3. Variety

From the outset it is important to build a variety of material and activity into the scheme. Combine individualized and class-based work and, if possible, some group-based work too. From the survey it appears that those schools which kept to a mainly class-based form of organization had difficulty in achieving genuine continuity for individual pupils. The weaker pupils tended to do the easier parts of the same range of topics as the abler pupils, and this often amounted to a succession of somewhat unsatisfyingly brief experiences. On the other hand the totally individualized systems quite often led to boredom on the part of both teachers and pupils since the general pattern of work was unvaried from day to day and week to week. In this situation there seemed a real need to limit the range of activities going on at any one time *and* to have a change in this range at periodic intervals. Organizing the scheme so that it embodied a variety of types of activity would avoid what we saw happening in some schools, where the organization and administration of a structured scheme absorbed the energies of the teachers to such an extent that the introduction of their own ideas and teaching activities into the scheme became almost impossible. One way of varying activity was seen at a school where the classes worked during successive fortnights on three kinds of work (see case study School A in Chapter VII).

4. Director material

The general development of the course over the years should be clear to all members of the department. It is probably best for staff to write director material rather than teaching material initially. These assignment sheets would suggest the study of sections from a variety of sources available in the classroom.

In this way the expenditure of large amounts of time on the production of actual instructional material, which may be no better than that which can be obtained commercially, can be avoided. A description of director material can be found in case study School C in Chapter VII.

Any basic, flexible scheme of this kind can be supplemented by assignments written by staff themselves. The process of injecting their own ideas into a scheme through school-produced assignments has proved to be of great value in the development of a mixed-ability scheme.

5. Sustaining innovation

For the innovation and development of mixed-ability teaching a cohesive team with a common purpose will need to be established through regular meetings, both formal and informal. In these meetings progress must be discussed, methods and materials evaluated and future plans made. Exchanges about such wide-ranging topics as the physical organization of classrooms, the grouping of children within a class, task assignments, provision for the most and least able, choice, assessment and record-keeping, the teacher's role, future types of grouping, successes and failures will need to take place in a free and candid atmosphere. The importance of the quality of leadership and example set by the head of department, and the professionalism and honesty of teachers within that department, cannot be overstated if this process is to be effective.

References and notes

1. See M. L. Goldberg, A. H. Passow and J. Justman, *The Effects of Ability Grouping*. Teachers' College Press, Columbia, 1966, chapter 1.
2. See J. Franseth and R. Kowry, *Survey of Research on Grouping as Related to Pupil Learning*. U S Office of Education, Washington, 1966.
3. See J. C. Barker Lunn, *Streaming in the Primary School*. National Foundation for Educational Research, Slough, 1970.
4. A. Yates (ed.), *Grouping in Education*, a Report sponsored by the UNESCO Institute for Education, Hamburg. John Wiley, 1966.
5. See R. Rosenthal and L. Jacobson, *Pygamalion in the Classroom*. Holt, Rinehart & Winston, New York, 1968, chapter 12.
6. See G. E. Whalley, 'Does transfer between streams work?', *Where*, Supplement 12: Unstreaming in the Comprehensive School. Advisory Centre for Education, 1968, pp. 14–17.
7. D. A. Pidgeon, *Expectation and Pupil Performance*. National Foundation for Educational Research, Slough, 1970.
8. E. Mayo, *The Social Problems of an Industrial Civilization*. Routledge & Kegan Paul, 1949, p. 64.
9. Board of Education, *Report of the Consultative Committee on the Primary School* [The Hadow Report]. HMSO, 1931, pp. 77–8.
10. Board of Education, *Report of the Consultative Committee on Secondary Education* [The Spens Report]. HMSO, 1938, p. 183.
11. Board of Education, *Report of the Committee of the Secondary School Examinations Council: Curriculum and Examinations in Secondary Schools* [The Norwood Report]. HMSO, 1943.
12. C. Burt, E. Jones, E. Miller and W. Moodie, *How the Mind Works*. Allen & Unwin, 1933.
13. L. M. Sturges, *Non-Streamed Science – a Teacher's Guide*. Association for Science Education, 1975, p. 5.
14. See G. V. Pape, 'Accident of birth', *Education*, vol. cviii, 16 November 1956, pp. 735–6.
15. See D. A. Pidgeon, 'Date of birth and scholastic performance', *Educational Research*, vol. 8, November 1965, pp. 3–7.

16. J. W. B. Douglas, *The Home and the School*, MacGibbon & Kee, 1964, p. 118.

17. See D. H. Hargreaves, *Social Relations in a Secondary School*. Routledge & Kegan Paul, 1967.

18. See J. Partridge, *Life in a Secondary Modern School*. Penguin Books, 1968.

19. See J. M. Ross *et al*, *A Critical Appraisal of Comprehensive Education*. National Foundation for Educational Research, Slough, 1972.

20. *Mixed Ability Teaching*, a Report on a Survey conducted by the Assistant Masters Association. AMA, 1974.

21. R. R. Skemp, *The Psychology of Learning Mathematics*. Penguin Books, 1971, pp. 37–53, 308–13.

22. P. A. Prettyman, 'Mathematics', in *Case Studies in Mixed-Ability Teaching*, ed. A.V. Kelly. Harper & Row, New York, 1975.

23. See N. Langdon, 'Smiling in the classroom', *Mathematics in School*, vol. 5 (No. 5) November 1976, p. 6.

24. D. W. Lingard, 'Teaching mathematics in mixed-ability groups', in *Teaching Mixed Ability Groups*, ed. E. C. Wragg. David & Charles, Newton Abbot, 1976.

25. See P. A. Bailey, 'Mathematics with mixed ability groups', *Forum*, vol. 13 (No. 1) Autumn 1970, pp. 10–12.

26. M. Young and M. Armstrong, 'Maths problems and solutions', *Where*, Supplement 5: The Flexible School, Autumn 1965, p. 16.

27. For a description and examples of this type of work, see P. A. Bailey, 'Psychology, organization and development', *Times Educational Supplement*, 4 October 1974, p. 68.

28. See A. W. Bell, D. Rooke and A. R. Wigley, *The South Nottinghamshire Project: Report 1973–75*, Notes, Material and Commentary. University of Nottingham, 1975, especially pp. 4–8.

29. See C. Banwell, K. Saunders and D. Tahta, *Starting Points*. Oxford University Press, 1972, pp. 67–151.

30. See D. H. Crawford, *The Fife Mathematics Project: an Experiment in Individualized Learning*. Oxford University Press, 1975, pp. 9–42.

31. S. L. Gunn, 'Teaching groups in secondary schools', *Trends in Education*, No. 19, July 1970, p. 3.

32. Department of Education and Science, *Mathematics, Science and Modern Languages in Maintained Schools in England*: an Appraisal of Problems in some Key Subjects by HM Inspectorate. DES, 1977, p. 10.

Part 2

Mixed-ability teaching in action

VI. The working group's inquiry

In 1976 a questionnaire was issued to all local education authorities in England and Wales asking for details of schools which were using mixed-ability teaching in mathematics in the 11–16 age range. The working group also asked for details of any persons (such as teachers, advisers, teachers' centre wardens) with experience in this field and active local groups producing materials for mixed-ability classes. The group then identified twenty-seven schools which represented a fair cross-section of current practice, in order that two-day visits might be arranged. All but one of these schools replied to an initial enquiry and were subsequently visited by members of the group. Those active local groups and persons with experience identified by the LEAs were also contacted and invited to provide the group with information about their activities.

During the two-day visits to schools various aspects of the teaching of mathematics to mixed-ability classes were investigated by talking to teachers and children, or by observing what happened in the mathematics department and the classroom. To build up an impression of the work, headteachers, heads of department and classroom teachers were given the opportunity to answer the following questions informally. It is suggested that these questions could also form the basis of a school's, or department's, self-assessment and evaluation procedure. There should be sufficient material here, suitably adapted to local circumstances, for a critical and careful appraisal to be made of most of the factors to be considered before embarking on mixed-ability teaching, and also to help to keep developments under constant review. Much that has been put to use here for mixed-ability teaching in mathematics could well be applicable to other departments too.

QUESTIONS PUT TO TEACHERS

The school and its environment

What is the age range of the pupils?

Is the school co-educational?

Does it cover the whole ability range?

What is the form entry?

How many pupils are there in the school? (Is there a sixth form?)

What is the background of the pupils?

Are there any ethnic minority groups in the school?

How old is the school and does this have any effect on staff recruitment?

How many feeder schools are there and what type are they?

To what extent do the feeder schools use mixed-ability teaching?

What is the degree and form of consultation with feeder schools?

How are children allocated to the school?

Does this affect the ability distribution?

What criteria are used to form the mixed-ability groups?

How long has mixed-ability teaching been operating in the school?

At what point do mixed-ability classes give way to a different type of organization?

What type of organization is then adopted?

Why is mixed-ability teaching given up at this point?

Courses and general organization of the mathematics department
What courses are offered?

What resources are available?

How are the rooms sited and arranged?

How are the groups formed?

How many pupils are there in each group?

How is mathematics timetabled? (For example, is it blocked?)

How many mathematics teachers are there (specialist or part time)?

How is the mathematics staff deployed?

What is the extent of team teaching (particularly with mixed-ability classes)?

What is the extent of in-service training for staff and student teachers (particularly with mixed-ability classes)?

Philosophy of the mathematics department

What are the aims and objectives of the department?

What are the reasons for having mixed-ability classes in mathematics?

What is the extent of mixed-ability teaching in mathematics?

Is the department alone in having mixed-ability teaching?

How long have mixed-ability classes been in existence?

At what point do you give way to other types of grouping?

Why do you give way to other methods?

What type of new organization is adopted?

How are the new groups formed?

Mixed-ability classes

Organization

How is the preparation and writing of material organized?

What is the effect on the teacher of this writing and preparation?

What provision is there for the extreme ends of the ability spectrum?

What is the degree and form of advance planning required for mixed-ability classes?

What is the policy on homework?

Teaching models

What type of class organization is used? Is it based on whole-class, individual or group work? Can you describe the classroom management of pupils.

What type of task is used?

What is the purpose of these tasks?

What kind of resources and materials are used? For example, are textbooks, work cards or worksheets used?

How are resources and materials managed in the classroom?

What type of task assignment is used (chosen by pupils, teacher directed or systematic) and why was this type of assigment adopted?

How flexible or structured is the approach?

What is the role of the teacher in the classroom? For example, does he spend most of his time managing, marking, instructing, or talking to pupils?

What kind of exchanges occur in the classroom? That is, does discussion between pupils and teacher—pupil discussion take place?

Course content and material

What is the course content for mixed-ability classes?

Is the material commercially published or school produced?

Why was this type of material adopted?

Is mathematics regarded as a body of knowledge or as an activity?

What kind of approach is adopted? Is it linear, or topic-based, or project-based, or investigatory?

Evaluation and assessment

What type of assessment is used?

How are these assessments recorded?

What is being assessed?

What procedures are there for finding and overcoming weaknesses of a child's mathematical development?

What is the relationship between mixed-ability classes and pupil groups for external examinations?

How do pupils perform in examinations?

How is the success or failure of the mixed-ability methods evaluated?

What is the effect of mixed-ability teaching on teachers' attitudes and expectations?

What is the department's evaluation of commercially produced material?

General considerations

What liaison is there between the mathematics department and other departments?

How do other departments view the teaching of mathematics to mixed-ability groups?

What problems were faced when mixed-ability teaching was adopted, and how were these problems overcome?

How do you see mixed-ability methods in mathematics developing in your school?

What advice do you have to offer to any teachers contemplating teaching mathematics to mixed-ability groups?

OBSERVATIONS IN THE CLASSROOM

Members of the working group involved themselves in the work of the classroom, taking particular note of the layout of the room, tasks that were made available, the activities of the pupils and the role the teacher adopted. The opportunity to study departmental schemes of work and syllabuses was taken and the material used with mixed-ability classes was studied in some detail. Group members were given the following checklist as a framework within which to record their observations in schools.

Teaching models

1 General description of a class.

a Desk arrangements. Give an account of the different activities and exchanges.

b Teacher occupation on a percentage scale.

c Pupils.
   i Itemize activities and tasks (giving numbers).
   ii Motivation: obtain the range of individual pupil's motivation by looking at: attentiveness, any signs of boredom; willingness to begin tasks; skimming through material; lack of comprehension.
   iii Range of ability: obtain evidence of the range by looking at individual pupils and examining their notebooks.
   Less able pupils: the number of non-readers, if there are any; the number of pupils continually asking questions of the teacher or of each other; any slow/poor writers.

Very able pupils: speed and accuracy of task completion; quality of finished material.

    iv Discipline: look for any continually troublesome pupils and the ways in which they attempted to disrupt the lesson.

    v Relationships: assess teacher—pupil relationships in the classroom (evidence of mutual respect, etc.); any desirable/undesirable features.

    vi Groups: describe the type of grouping; whether all members of a group contribute equally (dominant personalities/non-contributors/passive members).

2 Predominant teaching models.

Classify and add qualification and comments to the following criteria:
    Organization in the classroom
    Tasks and their purpose
    Resources
    Differentiation of tasks between different pupils
    The teacher's role both inside and outside the classroom
    Discussions taking place in the classroom.

3 Estimate the attainment of the possible desirable aims of teachers. Use above average/average/below average in comparing the whole set of schools being visited for their attainment of these aims.

   i Sound mathematical content and variety of tasks.

   ii Suitability of tasks for pupils (appropriate level of difficulty, interest and relevance).

   iii Continuity and development of the mathematical learning of individual pupils.

   iv Awareness by the teacher of individual pupils' progress.

   v Development of pupil's ability to organize his own learning activities.

   vi Mathematical discussions between pupils and between teacher and pupil.

4 Discuss with the head of department his priorities among these outcomes. Ask him to order them. Ask him if he has any other priorities.

Course content and material

1 General description of:

content;
material (e.g. commercially published or school produced);
the reason for the adoption of this type of material;
whether mathematics is regarded as body of knowledge or an activity;
the approach (e.g. linear, topic, project, investigatory).

2 Describe the material using the following headings:

a *The product*
type of material used (worksheet/work card/texts/workbook);
the purpose of the material (giving instructions/providing information/exercises/testing attainment);
the resources needed to produce materials.

b *The layout*
Size of sheet;
readability;
suitability for ability/age range;
visual interest, attractiveness;
appropriateness of illustrations to the intention;
ability to motivate.

c *Economy*
cost of production;
recovery for future use (storage and retrieval system);
durability, and how long it continues to be used.

d *Language*
balance of language (visual and written);
creation of subject—learner and teacher—learner barriers;
adaptability of material for different levels of conceptual development.

e *Context*

where it fits in the learning programme;

whether it is part of a planned course or series of isolated topics;

whether it increases learning opportunities in the classroom.

f *Outcome*

whether it restricts the teacher or pupil;

the type of learning it offers (e.g. the development of skills, techniques, concepts, relationships and strategies through exercises or exploratory tasks);

whether it is self-contained or offers the possibility of extension;

the type of question asked (e.g. recall, interpretation, application, calculation, classification, generalization, hypothesis construction);

the range of responses demanded of the pupil (e.g. written response, spoken response, discussion, use of other material or apparatus, investigation, reading for understanding);

where the pupils make these responses (e.g. on the worksheet, in a book, on paper, in a group report, in a display);

whether the pupil is motivated to go on to another card, sheet, extension work or other activities;

the marking demands of the material.

Using the information gleaned from observations and questions, informal reports for each school were prepared and considered at meetings of the group. After the initial survey, five schools which had special features, interesting problems, or exemplified good practice were identified and revisited. These revisits included a further investigation of various schemes, methods and materials and included schools in a variety of catchment areas using a range of teaching models. Three of these schools were used for the case studies in Chapter VII.

VII. **Three case studies**

In Part 1 of our report we have made some generalizations about current practice and have included a few examples to illustrate them. The purpose of this chapter is to describe the operation of mixed-ability teaching from a department point of view. Our three case studies are neither evaluative nor thorough since our visits were all too brief. The purpose of their inclusion is to give the reader a flavour of current practice in three schools.

SCHOOL A

This school, opened in 1964, was an 11–18 co-educational, nine-form entry comprehensive; there were 1450 pupils from a variety of backgrounds and the school served both rural and industrial areas. The school services exclusively eight feeder primary schools, all but one of which have mixed-ability teaching throughout. The pastoral organization is based on a house system, with a reception house for pupils in the first year.

The mathematics department had rejected individual learning as the solution to mixed-ability teaching and were trying class and group work. They were developing their methods in a climate of favourable conditions which include the following:

a a highly competent head of department;
b reasonable accommodation;
c support for the department by the headmaster;
d relatively small classes;
e availability of 'float' teachers;
f relatively few disruptive pupils;
g the removal of the most remedial pupils for special tuition;
h a well-established school;
i no apparent shortage of money;
j excellent reprographic facilities.

A high level of professional concern and commitment characterized the department. Mixed-ability methods in the first and second years were being developed in an atmosphere in which teachers were encouraged to work together, to talk and to share experiences. The ten full-time and two part-time teachers worked as a team, pooling efforts and ideas. Departmental preparation was such that any newcomer received helpful and extensive notes on the organization of the department which covered assessment, homework, 'floaters', workshops, resources, the structure of courses and the philosophy and approach to the scheme of work. Departmental meetings were held every four weeks, after school, to discuss forthcoming and past work and to share out tasks.

The head of department had established a philosophy of mixed-ability teaching before developing the organization to put it into operation. He was keen to ensure that children in different classes had the same mathematical education (this can be a problem in a large department). To achieve this consistency he believed that teachers should not be left to their own devices but must be included in a co-operative, shared effort.

In the scheme of work the content of the course was fully outlined and each topic/investigation had detailed notes and suggestions. The lesson plans given to teachers were far more detailed than the preparation any individual teacher could have hoped to produce. The staff seemed to accept that, although mixed-ability teaching is hard work for an isolated individual teacher, team-work can considerably lighten the workload and the adoption of mixed-ability classes is well justified in terms of stimulation and reward.

By providing this supportive organization, by his concern for the quality of mathematical education and by his good relationships with members of the department, the head of department had created an atmosphere in which teachers were encouraged to make a contribution. However, he was aware of the dangers of imposing a rigid structure which could cramp individual flair and inventiveness if the teacher did not take advantage of any flexibility offered.

He had innovated slowly, the schedule for the introduction of mixed-ability teaching having been:

1973   Entirely mixed-ability teaching in the first year. SMP work cards were adopted, with some topics being replaced by tasks from other sources.
1974   A new scheme of work using a variety of approaches and sources was developed and piloted with two classes in the first year.
1975   Half the first year used the new scheme.
1976   All the first year used the new scheme.

The second-year scheme was being introduced in the same gradual way:

1975   New scheme piloted with two classes.

1976   Half the second year used the new scheme.

Initially there were no great problems with the organization of resources. During this gradual process teachers took account of the pupils' responses to the material and were able to adjust the course content and organization of materials accordingly. Any problems which were likely to occur only did so on a small scale. New material was produced more cheaply in small numbers to begin with and teachers were able to try out new ideas and reject them if they did not work.

Some relevant aspects of the departmental operation will now be looked at in more detail.

Philosophy

The following extracts on aims and objectives, organization of classroom activity and writing are taken from the departmental handbook (see also *The South Nottinghamshire Project: Report 1973–75*).

1. Aims and objectives

Why teach mathematics?

(i)   Mathematics is a characteristic way of organizing our experience of the world which is employed wherever there is 'pattern' and 'structure'. As such it may enrich our understanding, enabling us to relate and interpret our experiences as well as giving pleasure. On a suitably wide definition much of the activity of a pre-school child might be described as 'mathematical' in character. As a subject, therefore, it lies at the heart of a great deal of human activity.

(ii)   Mathematics has important applications in many other fields, including science, engineering, social sciences, management, etc. We cannot say *what* mathematical knowledge will be useful to our students, but a significant proportion of them will need to learn *how* mathematics can be applied.

(iii)   Mathematics provides the most readily accessible form of problem-solving in the classroom (because it does not depend on a substantial body of pre-existing knowledge). This enables students to exercise and acquire confidence in their intellectual powers through a disciplined creative activity. Thinking independently and expressing arguments in a logical and ordered way does not always come easily; good habits can be acquired by being in a thinking situation, and by coming to recognize the general value of reasoning. One may also acquire some strategies which are more generally useful.

If these three arguments are a true basis for justifying mathematics in the curriculum, then they can both help us to define suitable objectives and to give an indication of the proper balance between different objectives, as well as providing some clues as to sources of motivation.

Knowledge objectives

These objectives relate to the topics on the syllabus and the content thereof.
(a) Knowledge of mathematical concepts, terminology, notation, facts, generalizations, methods and techniques.
(b) The ability to understand and interpret mathematical information presented in a variety of forms, and to be able to translate from one to another.
(c) The ability to apply knowledge and techniques to solve routine problems.

General objectives

These objectives are on a higher level and are more general in the sense that they do not relate to any specific content, but characterize mathematical 'activity'.
(a) The ability to select and apply techniques and strategies to unfamiliar situations.
(b) To understand what mathematics is involved in a situation, to symbolize and analyse it to find patterns.
(c) To argue inductively, make conjectures, verify and generalize.
(d) To provide 'proof': primitive justification, counter-examples, deductive argument.

Objectives related to attitudes and ways of working

(a) Developing appropriate attitudes to the subject, including confidence, attention, willingness to learn, and interest in the various aspects of mathematics – patterns, applications, problem solving, etc.
(b) Developing an appreciation of the significance of mathematics.
(c) Developing an ability to experiment, to write up accounts of activity (as well as results), and general formation of appropriate work habits.
(d) Developing an ability to formulate questions and extend problems.

In the past, mathematical education in schools concentrated heavily on knowledge objectives at the expense of other objectives. In recent years this has been criticized on two major counts. Firstly, rote learning of techniques often took place without either a proper basis of understanding or any sense of purpose. And secondly, mathematics as a creative activity was largely neglected. This led to a very limited view of the nature of the subject, an inability to make genuine applications and, in many cases, to a lack of interest.

Much more might be said on this matter, but our present purposes are adequately served if it is recognized that a balanced course can be provided only if all of the stated objectives are explicitly developed. Classroom activity must be continually measured against these objectives and, in the ultimate analysis, against the three primary reasons which we see as justifying mathematics as a compulsory element of the curriculum.

2. Organization of classroom activity

This is too wide a topic to develop fully here. All staff have been issued with a copy of the notes on this (from the South Nottinghamshire Project); they repay careful reading. The main points are:

(a) Tasks for the pupil
    (i)   experiments and investigations;
    (ii) programmed material for important concepts;
    (iii) practice of skills and techniques.
Of these, the first is undoubtedly of major importance, especially in the first three years (and still later for many pupils). It is best approached through the use of simple concrete materials.

(b) The role of the teacher
In groups with wide ability ranges the problem is to provide situations to which every pupil can respond at whatever level is valid for him. The purpose of the work cards and ways of using them are dealt with in some detail. The crucial role of discussion is discussed, with hints for developing it.

3. Writing

Whatever the way in which work is initiated, some sort of record may be required. Now when a technique is being rehearsed, i.e. the student is working through exercises, then the solutions are written down as the problems are solved. But when a real problem is being investigated for the first time, there are many vague thoughts, tentative jottings or experimental actions, before anything crystallizes. And a solution may appear in more appropriate form than marks on paper; for example, a film, a particular wiring of a circuit, a pattern of tiles and so on.

A write-up may be initiated after some activity merely by reminding the class what material is available and asking them to show in some way what sort of things they have been doing. In some cases it may be preferable to suggest some ways of going about this. (Try to explain to someone else . . . Make up some problems . . . How did you start? . . .) In any case, it is obviously important to discuss the nature of such work from time to time and to accept encouragingly, but not uncritically, early efforts.

How and where is work kept?

Who reads it? How is it assessed?*

Children like to see their own and others' work displayed on the walls and this needs to be encouraged (for example, some of the class could do an investigation write-up in the form of a wall-chart). Coloured backing-paper is available as well as large sizes of squared paper.

*C. Banwell, K. Saunders and D. Tahta, *Starting Points* (Oxford University Press, 1972), p. 38.

Resources

The department was situated in two areas of the school. Each area had storage facilities which were well organized and well used. Teachers could see at a glance what was needed, collect it and take it into one of the adjoining teaching areas. The storage spaces were large enough for the teacher to work in either for preparation, marking or group work. The range of available materials included those listed below.*

1. Games and puzzles

Angle (Peter Pan Playthings)
Connect (Galt)
Dominoes
Maestro (Peter Pan Playthings)
Match and Move (Spear's Games)
Mastermind (Invicta Plastics)

Multipuzzle (Invicta Plastics)
Space Lines (Invicta Plastics)
Tangrams
Think-a-Dot (Science Systems)
Tot Ten (Spear's Games)

2. 2D constructions

Angle indicators
Circles box
Compasses
Counters
Flexicurves
Mira (Cochranes)
Pantograph
Protractors
Rulers (30cm)
Set Squares $(30°/60°, 45°)$
Spirograph (Denys Fisher)

Shapes:
    acetate sheet
    geoboards (3 x 3 lattice, 4 x 4,
    5 x 5, 6 x 6, isometric)
    geostrips
    gummed polygons
    pattern blocks
    pegboards and pegs
Tiles:
    DIME tessellating tiles and
        pentagon triangles
    hexagons
    pentagons
    shape boxes

---

*For further details of suppliers, see pages 85 – 6.

3. 3D constructions

Constructostraws
Cubes: 1cm plain
     2cm coloured
     5cm plain
Empty chalk boxes
Headless matches

Multilink interlocking cubes (ESA)
Meccano
Solids box
Sticks
Straws and pipe-cleaners

4. Measuring, weighing, capacity

Calibrated beakers
Height measurer
Rulers (30cm, 1 m)
Scales
Tape measures

Trundle wheel
Weights
Wooden calipers
Wooden scale

5. Counting, attributes

Counters
Dienes' Logiblocs (ESA)
Headless matches

Punched cards
Two-sided counters

6. Number

Cuisenaire rods
Dienes Multibase Arithmetic Blocks
    Base 4, Base 5, Base 10 (ESA)
Electronic calculators
Hand calculator
Number balances

Number track
Prisms and cubes
Simple slide rules
Slide rules
Undyed Cuisenaire rods
Unifix (Philip & Tacey)

7. Statistics, probability

Circuit board
Decay dice
Dice

Playing cards
Probability Kit (E.J. Arnold)
Sample bottle

8. Paper

Large (20in x 30in)
 1cm, 2cm squared
 Backing (display) paper
 Card (different colours)
A4/A5
 Altair designs (Longman)
 Equilateral triangle
 Hexagons
 Lined
 Plain
 Polar

Cartridge paper
Kitchen paper

Spotty:
 square
 isometric
 for 3 x 3 geoboards
 for blocks of 16
Squared:
 1mm, 2mm, 5mm, 1cm, 2cm

9. Miscellaneous

Copydex
Drawing pins
Evostick
Felt pens
Filming equipment
Film loops
Guillotine
Gum

Paints
Paperclips
Pencils
Rice
Scissors
Sellotape
Staplers
Videotapes

Suppliers

E. J. Arnold
 Butterley Street, Leeds LS10 1AX

Cochranes of Oxford Ltd
 Leafield, Oxford OX8 ENT

Cuisenaire Company Ltd
 40 Silver Street, Reading, Berkshire

ESA Creative Learning Ltd
 School Materials Division, PO Box 22, Pinnacles, Harlow, Essex

Denys Fisher
 Thorp Arch Trading Estate, Wetherby, West Yorkshire

James Galt & Company Ltd
 Brockfield Road, Cheadle, Cheshire

Invicta Plastics Ltd
   Education Aids Division, Oadby, Leicestershire
Peter Pan Playthings Ltd
   Bretton Way, Bretton, Peterborough, Cambridgeshire
Philip & Tacey Ltd
   North Way, Andover, Hampshire
Science Systems
   175 Southampton Way, London SE5
Spear's Games
   PO Box 49, Green Street, Enfield, Middlesex

A school-based reprographic centre was also available to the department for the production of materials. Facilities included typing, photocopying, offset litho, roneo duplicating, thermal copying and the videotaping of television broadcasts.

Organization

Mixed-ability teaching operated in mathematics for the first year and half of the second year. Classes were blocked in half-year groups. There was permanent remedial withdrawal for a relatively small number of children, leaving approximately twenty-eight pupils in each mixed-ability class.

After the second year a different type of organization — setting — was adopted because the department was not yet confident enough to extend their approach further up the school. New groups were formed by using a test based on the NFER Basic Mathematics Tests DE and FG, and by teacher recommendations.

A characteristic of this school was the variety of teaching models used with each class. The three components of the course were: (a) investigation (whole-class activity), (b) number (individual work), and (c) workshop (group work). Most of the topics were designed to last two weeks and a detailed timetable was issued for each class. The course for the second year included the following topics:

Autumn term

Area	Statistics
Directed numbers	Transformations
Networks	Workshop
Number	

Spring term

Enlargement	Investigation
Finite groups	Number or workshop (three weeks)
Functions, operations	

Summer term

Investigation	Rotations
Number (three weeks)	Vectors and translations
Relations and graphs	Workshop (three weeks)

The components of the course will now be discussed in more detail.

(a) Investigation (whole-class activity)

This type of lesson was used for the learning of particular ideas and the development of some of the general strategies. These lessons occupied two-thirds of the time in the first year and about half the time in the second year. Notes on these teacher-introduced class topics were designed to put the activity into context, and to make suggestions about introductions, ways of working and ideas for extensions. The background notes were distributed to staff and progress was discussed at the monthly departmental meetings.

The tasks were very similar to those of the South Nottinghamshire Project (see Chapter VIII). Files on all class topics, each containing the necessary worksheets, etc. were available and maintained by the teachers on a rota, topic by topic. To enable material to be shared, each class needed to do each topic at a specified time. A timetable of activities for the first and second years was drawn up by the head of department, most of the topics lasting about two weeks. The first-year teaching notes on shape and symmetry are reproduced below (see also *The South Nottinghamshire Project: Report 1973–75*).

Shape and symmetry

Time allocation: six hours.

Content: Shapes, polygons (names), symmetry (line and rotation).

Equipment: (in kit) four shape boxes, sixteen 25-pin geoboards, rubber bands, Work cards 1–6.

General: All children will have done simple work on symmetry in their primary schools (ink blots, paper-folding and the like). The work here is to remind them of that, and to develop it from simply recognizing and drawing lines of symmetry towards some deeper mathematical ideas. (There may be some children who do not have these elementary concepts – they can be given the 'Symmetry' booklet to start with – but it is unlikely that there will be more than one or two in a class.)

Organization: There are two aspects to this topic (one using shape boxes and the other geoboards), each half of the class spending three hours on each aspect. This can be slightly tricky initially. Perhaps the best plan is to give out the shape boxes and Card I to the groups and let them get on with it while explaining the geoboard work to the other half. (If possible, it is probably best for the least able to do the shape boxes work first.)

1. Shape boxes

There are four boxes in each kit, so one box between four pupils is suitable. The first two cards are to allow some familiarity with the shapes to be gained, and to remind pupils about ideas of symmetry. Card 3 concentrates on rotational symmetry. Genuine explorations are needed here, and children should be encouraged to produce a large selection of designs in rough before drawing any of them in their exercise books. Discussions are important: from Card 3 ideas of rotational symmetry, and the fact that the patterns have no lines of symmetry, should be brought out. Card 4 directs attention to the individual shapes, as well as recalling the work on geoboards from last half term.

Less able children may only get this far, but most should tackle the important work on Cards 5 and 6. This is an investigation around symmetry, with some general results to be found. The question being asked is, 'What symmetries can different polygons have?' Quite a few children, especially the most able, will get through Cards 1–4 very quickly, but Cards 5 and 6, together with write-ups, should take at least two hours and a homework.

2. Geoboards

(a) Line symmetry

Each pair requires a 25-pin board and bands. A line is made across the board, and the problem is for one person to design a figure and the other to complete the picture to make the whole figure symmetrical about the first line. Some of the results should be recorded.

> 'What happens if the figure crosses the line of symmetry? (write about what you notice).'
> 'Try two lines of symmetry.'

Starting with a diagonal line is interesting. This can be made easier by working on a pegboard, with a chalk line drawn in; there one needs to concentrate more on the individual points rather than the whole figure. (This can be used to start off, before using geoboards at all, if desired.)

Pupils should be encouraged to describe what they did, and record significant results.

Triangular geoboards are available and would extend the range of possible symmetries.

(b) Rotational symmetry: halving the board

Previous work was concerned with line symmetry. This problem is intended to introduce the concept of rotational symmetry.

Initial discussion of the problem is desirable, since we must first establish what is meant by congruent (or 'equal') halves. (There is a film loop, *Let's Take Half* (Leapfrogs Group, 1977), which might say more than words can.)

> 'Use a rubber band to divide the board into two equal (congruent) halves.'
> 'Show the rest of the class.'
> 'How do you know they are equal?'

If the groups are then left to explore on their own, it is likely that many of the children will exhaust their ideas after generating about five examples. At this point the teacher can discuss the desirability of a systematic procedure. A useful general strategy is to vary an existing situation, e.g. keep part of a figure fixed and vary another part of it:

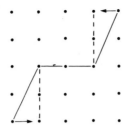

Most should then have little difficulty in finding fifteen examples. It is perhaps best *not* to let children go on to find as many ways as they can (there are 162 different ones).

Discussion on this activity should mention rotational symmetry — the concept needs to be made explicit. Centre of rotation may also be mentioned.

1. Making shapes with rotational symmetry. Identify the centre nail. Make a small shape in one corner. Complete the figure for rotational symmetry (again, working in pairs). Do this quite a few times and draw the best. (For the most able)

What happens when a figure has to be completed and it has to have both rotational (half-turn) symmetry and a line of symmetry? Make some, draw them and discuss the shape. (The final figure always has *two* lines of symmetry. Why?)

2. Quartering the board. This is similar to the work on halving, but is a useful extension as it introduces rotational symmetry of a different order.

3. Isometric boards. The same questions.

This kind of whole-class organization presented several problems. The difficulty of finding the kind of investigation which children can explore at their own level had largely been overcome. A still outstanding problem was related to ways of working. Children in the first year were unfamiliar with the approach and the teachers needed to train them to work profitably on their own, to 'keep their steam up', to take the initiative and to write up the activity. In the classroom the teachers found that their intervention and discussion were crucial factors in overcoming these problems. Children were encouraged to sit in groups and the furniture was rearranged if necessary. Teachers found that the time-limit of two weeks created problems of continuity, particularly for the less able pupil.

(b) Number (individualized work)

The purpose of this lesson was to develop computational understanding and skills. The units were based on the SMP work cards, together with booklets produced by the department. In the first year the topics covered were number, multiplication, fractions, decimals, division, number bases and measuring. In the second year, pupils did further work on the first-year topics and also ratio and percentage. In the first year each pupil was presented with a record card on which the topics were arranged as shown in Figure 3.

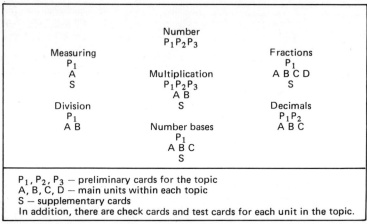

Fig. 3 First-year pupil's record card (School A)

Pupils were allowed some freedom of choice in the order in which they tackled the topics. They worked at their own rate through the cards; those who felt competent on any unit did just the check cards and test cards until they reached a level where they needed to do the whole set for that unit. Each child marked off each unit as it was completed. Some pupils liked to have each card within the unit marked on completion, others waited until they were ready to do the check card. No pupil was allowed to do the test card until the teacher had marked his check card.

At the time of the survey the head of department expressed concern about this aspect of the course. He felt there was a need to diagnose what children already knew and to offer appropriate work. However it was felt that the cards were often unsuitable for this purpose since the explanations were too linear, not giving the pupils the chance to think about the work and develop it. Although the cards provided an opportunity for the pupils to refresh their memories of various computations through practice, they did not enable deficiencies in understanding to be remedied effectively since they did not provide the teaching nor the discussion necessary for the correction of mistakes of memory or the filling of gaps in pupils' understanding. Concern was also expressed about the number work becoming an isolated part of mathematics (i.e. arithmetic). Number work needs evident and immediate application for pupils; the motivating factor of this cannot be underestimated. That being said, the pupils enjoyed these lessons, could see the value of them and were highly motivated, probably because of the similarity of this work to that of their primary school.

(c) Workshop (group work)

These lessons provided the opportunity, through investigations and experiments, for pupils to use concepts in unusual situations. They appeared to develop the pupils' ability to work on their own. They aimed to create an awareness of the occurrences of mathematics in everyday life and to promote pupils' ability to recognize and use general mathematical strategies such as classification and generalization. In the second year, number and workshops took up half the pupils' time.

A choice of activities was provided through topic books, investigations and a wide use of other materials. This provision enabled most pupils to get started on some mathematical activity. Sources include the Leapfrogs *Network* booklets and some DIME booklets (see Chapter VIII). The use of these materials in a workshop is described in one of the accounts of lessons in Chapter IV (Class D). Each teacher was issued with notes on workshops, extracts from which are reproduced below.

What is a workshop?

A workshop is an arrangement in the classroom that offers a free choice to pupils from a range of activities, most using equipment of some kind, many using topic books, work cards or worksheets. Some workshops have a wide variety of activities, others are built round a theme or concentrate on two or three topic areas. The feature common to all of them is that the pupil chooses for himself and so the role of the teacher becomes somewhat different from usual (see below).

In the autumn term the workshops are 'unrestricted', while in spring and summer they become more particular. Sometimes, during the middle of the year, workshop and number work goes on simultaneously. It follows that there will be a lot of different activities going on simultaneously. In the early spring term 75/76, it was noted what the children in class 2S were doing in one lesson (it was a mixed number/workshop block):

Table 1   Margaret and Caroline were using calculators to check some decimal work they had done. Heather and Harriet were on ratio cards.

Table 2   Andrew and Nicholas were plaiting solids. Jim was drawing a frieze using reflections and rotations. John and Alan were looking through the Leapfrogs *Links* book together.

Table 3   John was doing some work on fractions and Cuisenaire rods. Ralph was working out some decimal multiplication on a calculator.

Table 4   Lesley was doing some measuring. Marion was using a mirror card. Sarah was doing some 3D isometric sketching.

Table 5   Alison was working on percentage. Mandy was doing some fraction cards.

Table 6   John, Stephen and David were doing a statistics experiment.

Table 7   Valerie was doing some measuring. Gillian was doing nothing. Janice was designing some tiles.

Table 8   Kevin and John were on the back bench trying to follow the instructions for the desk-top computer to use it as a calculator.

Why workshops?

The following extract is taken from *Introducing the Leapfrogs Group*, a pamphlet issued by the group in 1975 [see Chapter VIII]:

There are, however, more positive reasons for designing a non-sequential set of activities. These arise out of the view that the best kind of learning is that in which the learner makes the subject-matter — its facts, techniques and ideas — his own. And this is best done by providing a wide variety of significant and potentially interesting activities and stimuli from which the learner can make a choice. Having made his choice he will learn from it what is significant to him at his particular stage of development. He is not being asked to learn material which, not having this kind of significance, would remain alien to him. (p. 4)

Thus we hope for increased motivation, and that the pupils will be able to work at levels appropriate for them.

There is also quite a lot of work that does not need to be formally taught — indeed, should not be formally taught. This largely consists of areas where experience is the important thing, where we want the pupils to have sufficient experience of certain things before we come to formalize them later on, but where there is no point in making children repeat the experience (which may have been acquired outside the classroom); examples might be 3D work, or reflections and mirrors. Thus a pupil who has inadequate ideas of chance can spend some time experimenting and gaining new insights.

The teacher's role

The use of these materials in the kind of context described implies possibly different but rewarding ways of working for the teacher. Freed from being only an instructor he may become more efficiently a guide and consultant. He is no longer the sole arbiter of content which is then expounded by him and received by the pupils. The content will be determined by the path that the pupils choose to take in response to the starting-points provided by the books. The teacher's role becomes that of facilitating the journey by providing discussions, questions, suggestions for other sources . . . (*Introducing the Leapfrogs Group*)

92

An instance from class 2S in 75/76 might be illuminating. John picked up a newspaper colour supplement that was lying, by chance, on the back bench (it was not part of the workshop materials). Its centre spread was a drawing showing modern warfare techniques

'I want to draw this,' he said. When I demurred, suggesting that it was not mathematics, he said, 'It's as mathematical as *this* chart,' and searched through the *Links* book to show me the dog classification chart.

'Tell me about it,' I said. And he explained how the drawing showed how things happened in sequence (first the planes come over, then . . ., then . . .). After some more talk I showed him a topic book on flow diagrams, and suggested that he copied the drawing at home and then next lesson produced a flow diagram of the process.

He arrived back the next day with the drawing *and* flow diagram, and then spent the next two lessons working through some of the flow diagrams in the topic book, producing one for starting a car and using a given one to construct an ellipse. (He found this quite hard – the book is really intended for fourth years – but he persevered, gaining experience in using protractor and compasses.)

It follows that the teacher needs to be flexible, and should not attempt to force his interpretation on pupils but assist them in carrying out their own intentions. Of course, the teacher needs to be familiar with the content of books, worksheets etc., to know what equipment is needed and where to find other pieces that might be required. But above all, it is vital to listen to and talk with each pupil.

Practical dangers

(i) Pupils sampling in a desultory way, trying something for a short time and then jumping on to something else. A good rule here is not to let anyone change activities until you have discussed the previous work with them.

A related danger is that of pupils doing a piece of work superficially, of not getting to ask the main question, or not being properly engaged with the problem. It needs stressing to the pupils (and it needs time to sink in) that we are not just doing quick little tasks and then jumping on to the next one. They will, fairly frequently, need encouragement to continue, especially in the early stages of working like this.

(ii) Pupils working at too low a level for their ability. The greatest danger is in copying from books. Pupils see an interesting drawing and, instead of producing something of their own inspired by it, simply do a copy from the book. They will need to be discouraged from this (although copying may, of course, be the right way to lead into the work sometimes).

Also to be guarded against is a tendency for pupils to do some low-level things they were expert at years ago: doing a survey, drawing block graphs of data, etc.

(iii) Crazes: someone makes a flicker book, does a survey, finds differences in fingerprints, and then everyone wants to do it. Some caution is needed.

Recording

A lot of work will be done in exercise books, a lot more on paper (with some big sheets for display – this is to be encouraged). We have prepared record books for each pupil (they are cut-down exercise books). It is a good idea for them to write some sentences on what they have done during the last five or ten minutes of each lesson.

Float teachers

The 'floater' played an important part in the success of the number and workshop lessons. He could take total responsibility for a group of less able children, either by extracting them to another room or remaining in the class in a consultative role. The decision about this was made between the class teacher and the floater and the children were told whom to consult and whom to ask for help. An important aspect of this provision was the continuing discussion between two teachers about the progress of each child. This generous staffing arrangement was partly recovered by having larger classes in the third, fourth and fifth years and by some teachers giving up their non-teaching periods. The departmental notes below describe the role of the floater.

Notes on floaters

General

The floater is attached to a pair of classes; the main purpose is to assist with the work of the least able children in those classes. This is seen as an alternative to withdrawing these children to a separate group. The floater will work almost entirely in the rooms with the two classes (these rooms are always adjacent).

Identifying the slow-learners

This should be a joint task with the class teacher. In the first two or three weeks of the autumn term, while the classes are working on class investigations, both teachers should try to pick out these children. There will be a test (NFER Basic Mathematics Test DE) before half term and a number diagnostic test before the first unit on number; these will help to identify other weaknesses and identify any slow learners that have been missed. The number of children picked out will vary from class to class but should not be more than 5–8 in a class.

Deployment of floater

The floater will be attached to each of the two classes for a fortnight at a time, always when the class is doing number work or workshops, and at other specified times. The other occasions are usually when the unit involves separate activities for different parts of the class (e.g. computing in the number patterns section or filming).

There are a few fortnights during the year when the floater is not allocated to a class; he can then be with a particular class by arrangement, be preparing materials, etc.

Working in the class

The children must of course be told that they are working with the floater. The floater then takes over responsibility for setting work, explaining, marking, and discussing work with these children. For the number work he needs to be familiar with the materials and methods for attempting to cope with fundamental difficulties; for workshops, to be as familiar as the class teacher with the range of materials and books.

Sometimes it is a good idea to put the slow-learners together in a group so that they can work together on a common topic; frequently pairs would be useful.

Reading

The amount of help needed with reading by the mathematically unable varies enormously. It is not a good idea to do all of the reading for a poor reader; in attempting it themselves they are getting some practice.

Reports and grades

The class teacher is responsible for all of the grades. He should consult with the floater about the reports of the slow-learners; it would be a good idea for the floater to write notes that could be incorporated into the reports.

Homework

Homework also had an important part to play. The department's policy shows ways in which homework can be integrated into the scheme of work.

Homework policy (first and second years)

Two homeworks per week are scheduled. Sometimes the notes refer to specific worksheets which provide tasks for homework and these should be set. However, at other times it is more difficult: when pupils are working on the cards, for example, they cannot keep them and take them home, and so cannot continue the work started in class.

Write-ups

One of the objectives of the course is to get children to write about what they have done. It is a useful part of an activity to get the children to describe as part of their homework what they have been doing in class during the day (this will not be needed if a major write-up — of an investigation, for example — is to follow; then, in any case, part of the write-up can be done at home).

Some caution is, however, needed here. Writing should not become a routine, and is perhaps best done when the class has been doing different things in the lesson. These mini-accounts provide a good way of helping with the problems of selecting material and describing mathematical activity.

Revision sheets

These are only appropriate to the second half of the year. There are a lot of duplicated revision sheets which can be used (and returned). There are only a small number of each (about six) for each pair of classes, so several different ones would have to be given out. (In any case, it is unlikely to be suitable for all of a mixed-ability group to have the same worksheet.)

Finishing off

Work started in class can sometimes be finished off at home (provided it does not involve materials, taking away worksheets, etc.). This is often very inequitable: the able children may have already finished before the end of the lesson, while the work may still take the less able a long time. Also, in many of our topics, the children will be working on quite different things. This solution needs to be used with caution.

Problems and puzzles

Two or three of these can often provide a stimulating homework, even for the relatively unable. There are several collections of these and we might be able to organize them for distribution.

The least able

They often need specific homework and are less able to cope with vague instructions. Since the floater will be seeing their work fairly regularly, it is possible to set them homework by writing in their books.

Summary

The features of the development of mixed-ability teaching in School A were gradual planned innovation, the use of a variety of teaching models and materials, the implementation of a well-defined departmental package, and formal and informal departmental discussions. This approach was adopted by the head of department to try to achieve quality of work and consistency of mathematical education across all classes in a large school.

SCHOOL B

This schools was an 11–18 co-educational, eight-form entry comprehensive for 1140 pupils. The school is situated on the outskirts of a northern industrial town in a mixed dormitory and mining community. Originally it was a secondary modern school but has been fully comprehensive for the last five years. The headmaster had established a policy of mixed-ability teaching over the last five years and at the time of the survey all subjects were taught to mixed-ability groups in the first and second years. There are five feeder schools, all of which have mixed-ability classes.

96

Philosophy and aims

The philosophy of the department was to make maths enjoyable, to stretch the able pupils and to develop the potential of all pupils. This philosophy is expressed in the document on aims and ideas drawn up by the head of department some years ago.

Aims and ideas

Members of the mathematics department are encouraged to experiment.

The work must be stimulating, realistic and as true to life as possible. Try and draw on the children's everyday experiences. Get away from the textbook: use charts, graphs, diagrams, models, apparatus and a practical approach whenever possible.

Make the children aware of the maths around them in everyday life. Encourage them to record, discover and present information in various forms (graphs, for example) and to draw their own conclusions from this information.

The syllabus must be expressed with understanding and imagination. Try a fresh approach. Make the subject appeal. Make it interesting.

There must be less mechanical teaching: the children must be encouraged to discover rules for themselves and we must avoid pounding away at tables and mechanical processes all the time. It is more important that a liking and enjoyment for maths is induced and that the basic principles are practised in some of the more interesting and wider fields of the subject.

Mathematics is not a static thing; it is progressive and plays a vital part in our lives. We should try to think in these terms when we are teaching.

At times the work must be of a practical nature and as varied as possible; working in pairs or groups must be encouraged. Observation of experiments of a practical nature can be recorded, charts and diagrams drawn and deductions made from these experiments.

We must try to ensure that the pupils have both the understanding of fundamental mathematical concepts and the ability to apply basic calculations appropriately and accurately to realistic situations. We must try to give the pupils a wider experience of maths in as attractive a form as possible. The main aim is to help the pupils understand, and relate themselves to, some of the mathematical problems of the world outside the classroom.

Children's work as well as teacher's work must be on display. The room should be colourful, attractive and exciting. Working apparatus could be in evidence. Collections of shapes to be encouraged. The classroom should be interesting and appealing.

The enthusiasm and professionalism of the head of department was a major factor in achieving these aims. He had been at the school for about twenty years and had established a stable department. He obviously influenced and inspired children and the other members of the department with his dedication to teaching and love of mathematics. He had developed a very personal approach based on a knowledge of individual children, good personal relationships and the realization of the importance of communication.

In the classroom he believed that the teacher should excite the children through his own personality and by choosing work which applied mathematics to as many realistic situations as possible in an interesting way. He also believed that children should realize that what they were doing was worth while. He demanded a great deal from his staff and there was no doubt that the example he set influenced the whole department, every member giving a positive response to his lead.

Resources in use

These included a wide variety of textbooks, programmed learning booklets and topic booklets. Although there were plenty of books to choose from they were quite limited in style, having a mainly traditional content, and included the following:

Adam, J. W. and Beaumont, R. P. *More Practice in Mathematics*, Books 5 and 6. Schofield & Sims, 1974.

Bell, Stuart E. (ed.) *Mathematics in the Making* series, Longmans, 1970–71.

Channon, J. B., Smith, A. M. and Head, H. C. *New General Mathematics*, Books 1 and 2. Longmans, 1970.

Harris, Roy
Angles (Clearway Programmed Books). Methuen, 1965.
Triangles (Clearway Programmed Books). Methuen, 1965.

Marshall, G. *A World of Mathematics*, Books 1–6. Nelson, 1970–72.

Shaw, H. A. and Wright F. E. *Discovering Mathematics*, Books 1 and 2. Edward Arnold, metric edition, 1975.

There was a central maths area of four classrooms, three of which opened on to an open area at the head of a stairway; other rooms were used elsewhere in the school. The rooms were spacious and the tables were arranged in formal rows. A feature of the rooms was the extensive displays of pupils' work on pinboard.

Organization

The mixed-ability classes in the first and second years contained, on average, thirty pupils and were timetabled in blocks; this allowed children to have a change of teacher under some circumstances. The arrangement was used to alleviate discipline problems. The five full-time and two part-time teachers were timetabled for classes covering all years and all abilities. The timetable arrangements for Years 1, 2 and 3 were:

Year 1   Mixed-ability classes were blocked in half-year groups for five lessons per week. Very remedial pupils were removed for specialist teaching.

Year 2   Same as year 1.

Year 3   Four lessons per week in two blocks as shown below. Remedial provision as in previous years.

Block 1
One potential O-level class
Three mixed-ability potential CSE classes;

Block 2
One potential O-level class
Three mixed-ability potential CSE classes.

The new groups in the third year were formed on the basis of a test given at the end of the second year and on teachers' recommendation. In effect, the potential O-level candidates were 'creamed off' in years 3, 4 and 5 and the remainder followed a Mode III CSE course. The head of department gave the following reasons for segregating this group:

a   the extent of the O-level syllabus;

b   the more able need a different course which will stretch them fully;

c   the large number of pupils in a mixed-ability class might hinder the progress of the more able. The demands of the average and less able might lead to the more able being neglected.

Content of course and teaching method

Years 1 and 2

In the first two years teachers had to cover certain themes, for example: number, shape, graphs, modern maths (e.g. number bases, sets, etc.), the circle, the triangle. The underlying assumption was that each child could find something to interest him within a theme. There was no one set of books; teachers had found the adoption of a single text very limiting. At least fifteen different texts were available and were deliberately chosen for their attractive format, simple language and good basic mathematical principles. (Some of these books have been mentioned in the description of Class C's lesson in Chapter IV, and also on page 98). Teachers selected what they wanted from the materials available. There was freedom for the teacher to develop his or her own course but at the same time each one seemed fully aware of what others were doing.

The teaching model is a mixture of group, individual and class work, although the predominant pattern was group and class work. For example, the pattern might be:

a Individual work: work cards and programmed learning books.

b In groups: four or five children in a group. For example:
Group 1 doing pure number work;
Group 2 doing simple equations:
Group 3 using geometry matching cards;
Group 4 doing polyhedra;
Group 5 doing fractions, aided by fraction dominoes.

c As a whole class: there were times when the whole class worked on the same topic. For example:

   i Sampling in statistics when a whole-class result was required.

   ii Work on shape recognition, cutting out shapes and class discovery of properties.

   iii On a theme like number, the following topics were able to be pursued:

      magic squares
decimal numbers (supermarket bills etc.)
roman and arabic numbers
positive and negative numbers
squares and cubes (use of tables)
co-ordinates
vectors
matrices
sequences
circles
angles.

The approach was flexible, the degree of flexibility depending on the particular teacher. Some teachers were more obviously concerned with having all pupils doing the same thing at the same time; in most cases these were the least experienced members of the department. The head of department was constantly encouraging them to maintain interest by regularly changing content, activities and teaching styles, although in practice this variety was difficult to achieve with all teachers.

Discussion between teacher and pupil was a feature of most of the lessons, and some teachers made a positive attempt to talk to every child in the class; with double lessons this task was not impossible. These exchanges were not limited to pupils who were stuck but reflected the teachers' concern in getting pupils to talk about what they were doing. As a general observation, the teacher appeared to spend half his time on administration, organization and the provision of new work and the remaining half on working and talking with the children.

The assessment of children's work tended to be informal and impressionistic, being based on personal knowledge and good relationships with the children. The children's books were kept as a record of progress. A noteworthy feature of this school was the high standard of presentation of work both in exercise books and in wall displays. The pupils were clearly confident when they were preparing display material to be pinned up on the walls. It was obvious that they had acquired a knowledge of display techniques and they were able to set out the required piece with quiet efficiency.

The criteria on which a teacher based his assessment of a pupil's work were:

general attainment on topics covered;
presentation of work (which was very important in this school);
general understanding, established by discussion with the pupil.

It was the responsibility of the classroom teacher to identify strengths and weaknesses in a child's mathematical development and to provide individual work to cater for any obvious needs. The flexibility of the system allowed for this although the quality of the work provided varied from teacher to teacher.

Years 3, 4 and 5

During these years the potential O-level candidates followed a traditional mathematics course taught on formal lines. The remaining mixed-ability groups worked in much the same way as the first and second years by following a very flexible Mode III CSE course, the syllabus of which is reproduced below. A noteworthy feature of this course is the large part played by course-work in the final assessment.

CSE Mode III mathematics

The main aim of the course is to give the pupils a good mathematics background and provide a wide range of mathematical ideas which they can investigate and pursue so that they can then apply these discoveries to realistic situations. The scheme will not be narrow but will be wide open to experiment and imaginative thinking. It will largely be based on shapes organized in themes.

Themes

1. The triangle

Programmed learning course.
Types of triangle and their construction.
Finding missing angles.
　　'Discover formula for finding the area of a triangle.
　　Cut out triangles, make up your own problems and find their areas.'
　　(Involving vulgar fractions and decimals.)
Triangles in everyday life; illustrated with cuttings.
The right-angled triangle; Pythagoras.
　　'Find missing sides. Use a log book as a piece of apparatus.'
How to look up squares and square roots.

Congruency
Defining
Establishing rules for congruency, e.g. SAS, ASA, RHS.
Follow up and prove that one angle equals another angle.

Similarity
Meaning.
　　'Cut out triangles that are simlar.
　　Discover that the corresponding sides of similar triangles are in the same ratio.
　　Use similarity to find the lengths of the sides of triangles.'

Trigonometry
The right-angled triangle.
Introduce ratio (e.g. tangent, sine, cosine).
Find missing sides and missing angles in right-angled triangle.
Problems based on above.

2. The circle

Disc diagrams involving use of protractors: pocket money, timetables.
Introduce words 'circumference', 'diameter', 'radius'.
　　'Find circumference of various round objects by measuring.

　　Divide C by diameter.
　　Discover that $\dfrac{C}{d} = 3\frac{1}{7}$. By cross multiplication $C = 3\frac{1}{7}d$.'

Finding the circumference of various wheels – toy wheels, table-mats, tin lids, etc.
Lead on to area of circles.
Link up with cylinders by finding surface area of cylinder.
'Make your own cylinder. Find the volume and surface area.'
Curve stitching.
The spirograph.
Construction of cardioids, etc.

Introduce geometry: segments of circles.
Work on angles in the same segment.
Cyclic quadrilaterals; angles in a semi-circle.
Finding length of arcs.
Finding area of sectors.
Area of circular borders (difference of two squares).
Volume of metal used in pipes.

3. Polygons

The quadrilateral family: square, rectangle, rhombus, parallelogram, trapezium.
'Construct, cut out, examine their properties and angles. Recognize corresponding, alternative and supplementary angles.
Make discoveries (e.g. different ways of finding the area of a rhombus).
Finding missing angles. Discover formula for areas.'
Work with plastic hexagons and pentagons.
'Draw round them, cut them out, examine their angles.
Find out how to construct them and discover their properties.'
Shapes used in everyday life.
Lead into problems, e.g. 'The interior angle of a regular polygon is $108°$ – how many sides has it?'

4. Solid geometry

Regular solids – polyhedra.
Solids with length, width and thickness are given the name polyhedron. Each surface or face is a polygon and, even though there are many, only five are regular. Investigation into the five polyhedra, making nets, then their solids: tetrahedron, hexahedron, octahedron, icosahedron, dodecahedron.

5. Graphs

A graph is a mathematical picture.

Use as much up to date and realistic material as possible.
  Disc diagrams
  Pictographs
  Block graphs
  Straight-line graphs
  Time and distance graphs (work from road maps and AA books)
  Simultaneous equation graphs
  Quadratic equations.

103

It is essential that pupils can put down information and record it in graph or picture form. They should also be able to make deductions and read information from graphs.

6. Theme on the home

Decimal currency; shopping; the cost of living
Interest
Buying and selling
Profit and loss
Household accounts
Cheques and cheque books
Mortgages
Rates and rent
Wages and salaries
Hire purchase
Car insurance
Holidays.

7. Topics using programmed learning booklets

Triangles
Angles and polygons
Indices and directed numbers
What base?
A use of ratio
Direction and bearings
Ratio and percentage
Factors and quadratics
Number bases and the binary system
Graphs
Sets and relations
Networks
Statistics.

It is advisable that pupils work through at least two of these programmed courses during their two-year CSE course.

8. Theme on number

History of number
Roman and arabic numbers
Squares and cubes
Cubes and cube roots
Reciprocals
Number patterns
Directed numbers — indices
Number bases
Vectors
Matrices
Statistics (mean, mode and median).

Work to be moderated

1 Two years' course-work;
2 programmed learning courses;
3 internal examinations;
4 one mathematical topic.

Summary

The teachers were generally keen and happy, and appeared to get on well together as a team. In the department there was maximum teacher autonomy within flexible guidelines. The system relied heavily on the teacher and his ability to develop the work on a theme basis. There were plenty of books to choose from, although they were limited in style. There was a distinct lack of investigative or open-ended work for children, most of the work being closed. However, the head of department was concerned that all teachers were extending pupils and were offering them possibilities of development. With an emphasis on formal teaching this might not always have been achieved. Most of the activities were heavily teacher directed with little choice for the pupil.

Most of the assessments were informal; the teacher got to know the pupils well by regularly checking and marking work. A characteristic of the school was the high quality of written work insisted on by the head of department and this was reflected in the standard of displays around the walls of the classrooms.

By developing their own Mode III CSE syllabus, with a high degree of course-work assessment, teachers in the department were able to continue thier mixed-ability teaching methods with classes remaining after the potential O-level candidates had been selected.

The success of School B was a direct result of the enthusiasm and charisma of the head of department, and his continued encouragement of the use of a variety of materials and teaching styles in the classroom. Other factors such as the accommodation, the stability of staff, the general availability of good reprographic facilities in the school, the children's positive response and obvious enjoyment of the subject, and the removal of the very remedial pupils were a help in achieving this success.

SCHOOL C

This school was a 13—18, co-educational, six-form entry comprehensive of 730 pupils with a rural catchment area with a twenty-mile radius. The two middle-schools used mixed-ability teaching; the majority of pupils from these schools progress into the high school, but some pupils were 'creamed' by a nearby public school and a grammar school. Mixed-ability teaching had been

105

operating in the school for twelve years. The school began as an 11–18 comprehensive, but the first two years were phased out and the school became 13–18 in 1977.

At the time of the survey the pattern of organization was:

Lower year (13–14-year-olds)
Mixed-ability classes, individually timetabled.

Middle year (14–15-year-olds)
Pupils may choose none, one or two options from the following courses (all taught in mixed-ability groups):

Mathematics. Seven groups, blocked three and four (O level and Mode III CSE)
Statistics. One group (O level and Mode III CSE)
Computer studies. One group (O level and Mode III CSE).

Upper year (15–16-year-olds)
(Four forms in the year group at the time of the survey.)

Mathematics.
    One O-level group extracted on the basis of teacher recommendation and class tests.
    Three mixed-ability groups for Mode III CSE.
Statistics. One group (O level and Mode III CSE).
Computer studies. One group (O level and Mode III CSE).

In all years mathematics was timetabled for three fifty-five minute lessons a week and was mostly taught in a four-room suite. Four full-time and three part-time teachers, including a deputy head and senior mistress, were involved in the teaching. The four full-time teachers, only one of whom had any length of experience, worked closely as a team and were all involved in the mixed-ability work although there was some delegation of responsibility for developing the various courses. The head of department encouraged informal discussion to mull over problems, activities, investigations, suggestions for extensions and evaluation of materials. Formal departmental meetings were concerned with assessment, grades, course-work, the evaluation of topics and more practical issues such as the use of the capitation allowance. In view of the extent of teacher autonomy and the flexibility of approach the department felt it was essential for discussion and inter-departmental co-operation to take place; otherwise each teacher would not have been aware of the developments taking place.

Philosophy, organization and course content

In developing mixed-ability courses the head of department saw social integration as of paramount importance. His aim was to keep standards of work and presentation high by ensuring that children were participating to the best of their ability. A stimulus was given to the work in mathematics in the following ways:

a by destroying the fallacy that certain skills are sacrosanct, by cutting down on content and providing more exploratory work;

b by removing some of the formality which is often used to teach concepts, skills and techniques;

c by encouraging the use of mathematical strategies and concepts in unusual situations;

d by providing more time for investigation work, offering the pupils the chance to use their mathematical ability in different ways;

e by replacing excessive rote practice with exercises more relevant to the pupils' experience.

No teaching notes as such were available but a list of topics for the lower year and CSE Mode III schemes of work were issued to the teachers. The CSE schemes of work also contained statements about aims and assessment. As the CSE Mode III syllabuses were an integral part of the mixed-ability work they, as well as notes on the topics for the lower year, are reproduced below in their entirety.

Topics for lower-year mixed-ability groups

The following list has been kept as brief as possible so that teachers will have some freedom to include in the lower-year course topics of their own choice. The list is not necessarily compulsory for all pupils, since some of the topics may not be suitable for the weakest. It is reasonable, however, to expect the large majority of lower-year pupils to be familiar with the topics listed, thereby giving some common ground for middle-year courses. The more able pupils ought, of course, to tackle the listed material and more advanced work.

Some of the topics may well have been dealt with by the middle schools and will need little, if any, reinforcement. In some instances, however, it may be useful to give pupils a different viewpoint on material with which they are already familiar. Calculators will obviously be helpful in many of the topics and their use should be encouraged. The most important topics are marked with an asterisk (*).

*Approximation, estimation**
Pupils should be encouraged to estimate answers and to use calculators critically. Decimal places and significant figures.

*Directed numbers**
+, −, x, ÷.

*Squares and square roots**
Using calculators and three-figure tables. Other work on indices as required.

*Basic algebra**
Using letters to represent numbers. Adding, subtracting, multiplying and dividing simple algebraic expressions (e.g. $3a$ x $2a$, $5t^2 \div t$). Simplifying. Coefficients, brackets, powers. Try to introduce algebraic forms of expression in other areas of the course.

*Solving simple equations and inequalities**
Solved by 'balancing' rather than flow diagrams. Level of questions in SMP Books E and F about right for most pupils.

*Mappings and graphical representation of mappings**
Graphing equations and inequalities. Straight line graphs, 'steepness', easy curves. Domain, range, image. Both types of notation (e.g. $y = x + 2$, $y > x$, $x \rightarrow x^2$, $x \rightarrow \frac{1}{x}$, $x \rightarrow \tan x$).

Simple shapes and solids
Properties of triangle, parallelogram, rhombus, cuboid, etc.

Area of simple shapes
Appreciation of areas, units used. Areas of rectangle, triangle, parallelogram, etc.

Volumes of simple solids
Appreciation of volume, units used. Volume of cube, cuboid, etc.

*Simple geometry of circle**
Tangent; patterns resulting from angle properties; cardioid, etc.

*π, area and circumference, volume of cylinder**
3.1 probably accurate enough for π.

*Reflection, rotation**
Practical and formal work, combining operations, use of overhead projector.

*Translation**
Translation linked with bearings.

*Enlargement, similar figures**
Ratio. Corresponding changes in length, area, volume.

Pythagoras
No proofs but demonstrations. Link with square roots.

Tangent of angles
Finding sides and angles. Three-figure tables.

Vectors and simple vector algebra*
Link with co-ordinates, translation. + and − vectors, parallelogram rule, x scalar.

Matrices and matrix operations*
Familiarity with matrices related to networks, traversibility, tabulating data, etc.

Simple probability*
Practical and formal work. Tree diagrams for combined events.

Statistics/Computing
Taster courses for middle-year options.

CSE Mode III mathematics

1. Introduction

Pupils at the end of their third year are able to select which mathematics course or courses they wish to follow for a further two years. They are able to make their choices from the following: computer studies, mathematics, statistics.

Some pupils will therefore opt for more than one course and their reasons for choosing to follow a particular course or courses may vary considerably. The statement of intent outlined below is for the mathematics course, which has been designed to cater for pupils of widely differing abilities and aptitudes. Some pupils who begin this course will be entered for the Joint Matriculation Board GCE O-level Mathematics (Syllabus C) examination at the end of their fifth year, but the majority of pupils who begin the course will be entered for assessment for a CSE grade. For these reasons the nature of the course is deliberately open-ended to allow for a diversity of interests and talents.

2. Aims

Our intention throughout the course is to provide situations in which pupils of all abilities will have the opportunities to derive enjoyment and satisfaction from mathematical work. In particular, our aim is to develop clarity of thought and expression, the application of mathematical principles to a given situation, deductive reasoning and logical thinking, creativity in problem-solving situations and a general appreciation of number, pattern and shape. This may be done through oral work in class, written work and practical work. The general approach to the syllabus will be intuitive, inductive and practical, utilizing to the full opportunities for pupils' discoveries through experience and experiment.

3. Topics

The number of mathematical topics covered by each pupil will vary, as will the depth or degree of complexity to which the topic is studied. The following list is intended as a guide to the main areas of study, but is not intended to be taken as a detailed syllabus. It is envisaged that many pupils will cover a number of related topics not listed below, but all pupils entered for assessment for a CSE grade will have dealt, at some level, with the following:

(a)   Sets and operations upon them.
(b)   Mappings and functions.
(c)   Number systems. Natural numbers, integers, fractions, rational and real numbers.

(d)   Arithmetical and algebraic techniques. Measurements. Computation. Accuracy, estimates and tolerances.
(e)   Solution of equations.
(f)   Matrices.
(g)   Geometry of regular shapes and solids, including symmetry, congruence and similarity. Transformation geometry.
(h)   Scalar and vector quantities.
(i)   Trigonometry. Sine, cosine, tangent and solution of right-angled triangles. Three-dimensional problems.
(j)   Probability.
(k)   Elementary statistics. Representation of data, measures of central tendency and dispersion.
(l)   Graphs and their interpretation.

4. Assessment

Assessment will be carried out continuously throughout the courses and will be based on course-work and project-work undertaken by pupils.

Course-work. This will be set throughout the first five terms of the course and will comprise a variety of tasks, largely of a problem-solving nature, some of which may require a practical or partly practical solution. Some of these tasks will involve work on the topics already mentioned while others will be of a more open-ended and investigative nature intended to stimulate mathematical curiosity and inventiveness and to encourage the development of problem-solving procedures and strategies. There will be no fixed time limit for this work and pupils will be encouraged to seek out and use suitable references. Discussion between teacher and each pupil about his course-work will take place and this discussion will contribute towards the teacher's assessment of the pupil's ability to handle a specific task. Other aids to this assessment such as tests, essays, etc. may be set at the teacher's discretion.

Project-work. This will be carried out in the fifth and sixth terms of the course. It may be a piece of work of the pupil's own choosing or a topic suggested by the teacher. The project may be an extension to a piece of work covered earlier in the course or may be some topic which has not been dealt with previously but is of particular interest to the pupil. The project will be carried out on an individual basis and may be practical or academic in nature.

The weightings for the assessment will be:

course-work   80 per cent
project work   20 per cent.

On assessing pupils' work, teachers will use the following criteria:

(a)   depth of knowledge and information;
(b)   degree of competence in using basic skills and techniques;
(c)   capacity to understand problems, to formalize them in mathematical terms and to develop and extend reasoning;
(d)   ability to reason creatively in mathematics;
(e)   ability to apply appropriate concepts to unfamiliar mathematical situations.

It is of course realized that the emphasis given to these criteria will vary according to the nature of the task.

CSE Mode III statistics

Reference should be made to the introduction of the school's CSE Mode III mathematics Statement of Intent, where some general comments appertaining to this statistics course are made.

1. Introduction

This is a course catering for pupils of widely differing abilities. Some of those entering the course at the beginning of the fourth year will be entered for the Associated Examining Board's GCE O-level examination at the end of their fifth year, but the majority will be entered for assessment for a CSE grade.

2. Aim

To give a basic knowledge of statistical ideas, relating them as far as possible to the interests of the pupils.

3. Topics

The following topics will have been covered by all pupils, although the depth or degree of complexity to which the topic has been studied will vary. Where possible there will be emphasis upon practical work.

(a)   Collection and representation of data. Classification and tabulation; diagrammatic and pictorial representation of data.
(b)   Misuse of statistics − distorted data.
(c)   Frequency distributions; histograms and frequency polygons. Normal and skew distributions.
(d)   Sampling and bias. Design of questionnaires.
(e)   Averages: arithmetic mean, median and mode. Weighted averages.
(f)   Dispersion: range, interquartile range. Mean deviation, standard deviation. Cumulative frequency distributions, cumulative frequency graphs. Estimation of medians and quartiles from ogives.
(g)   Scatter diagrams; graphical treatment of regression and correlation. Calculation of equations of regression lines in the form of $y = mx + c$. Coefficient of correlation. Rank correlation.
(h)   Index numbers.
(i)   Elementary analysis of time series, moving averages.
(j)   Probability: experimental and theoretical probability; combining laws of probability.
(k)   Simple treatment of permutations and combinations.

4. Assessment

Assessment will be carried out continuously throughout the two-year course, and will be made up as follows:
(a)   Objective tests. These tests, requiring written answers, will be given without warning throughout the course. The frequency of the tests will vary. Each test will carry a time-limit and pupils will not be allowed access to reference books.
(b)   Course-work. This will comprise worked problems and theoretical ideas investigated by the pupils on their own.

(c) Practical work. This will consist of written up experimental work based upon the theory covered.

The weightings for the assessment will be:

objective tests   40 per cent
course work   30 per cent
practical work   30 per cent.

CSE Mode III computer studies

Reference should be made to the introduction of the school's CSE Mode III mathematics Statement of Intent, where some general comments appertaining to this computer studies course are made.

1. Introduction

This course caters for pupils of widely differing abilities, although the majority are of average or below average ability. *All* pupils entering this course at the beginning of their fourth year will be entered for a CSE grade at the end of their fifth year. Many of these pupils will concurrently be studying mathematics (either to GCE O level or for a CSE grade). Some pupils may follow their computer studies course by studying for the AEB GCE A-level computer science examination in the sixth form.

2. Aims

(a) To study the history of calculating devices and the development of the computer.
(b) To give pupils a broad understanding of how a computer works.
(c) To teach pupils how to use a computer.
(d) To study applications of computers.
(e) To analyse the role and effect of the computer in modern society.

3. Topics

To realize the aims stated above, the course has been divided into five main areas of study.

(i)   *History of calculation.* A study of the development of calculation, from the earlier number system to third-generation computers. Including: logarithms, the slide rule, adding machines and mechanical calculators, and punched-card equipment. In particular the contribution made to this development by John Napier, Blaise Pascal, Joseph Jacquard, Charles Babbage, Dr Herman Hollerith and Dr John von Neumann.

(ii)   *How a computer works.*
    (a)   Hardware:
        A study of the basic components of a computer including the following: central processor, arithmetic unit and console control; core storage, magnetic tape and magnetic disc storage; punched paper tape and punched cards, line printer, MICR [magnetic ink character recognition], visual display and light pen, digital plotters, computer terminals.

112

(b) Software
Program languages. Language translation, compilers. Operating systems.

(iii) *Computer programming.* The need for clear logical thinking. Breaking a problem down. Flowcharting. The use of a simple machine code. The development of program languages. A good working knowledge of one such language.

Pupils will be expected to write a number of computer programs to solve simple problems and/or process data on topics which interest them. These programs will be written in: either *(a)* ALGOL, and will be processed by the Lancaster University Computer Department on their ICL computer; and/or *(b)* FORTRAN, and will be processed by the Department of Computing and Control at Imperial College, London as part of their Computing in Schools project.

(iv) *Computer applications.* A study of the scope and limitations of computers. Scientific, industrial and commercial applications. Data processing. The organization of a computer department. Computer personnel.

(v) *Social implications.* The fear and misunderstanding evoked by computers. Computer use and automation; increased leisure time. Analogies with the past (the Industrial Revolution, mass production). Redundancy. The control of people and the invasion of privacy. The impact of computers in the field of education. The future: science fiction, and the ideas of George Orwell and Aldous Huxley.

4. Assessment

Assessment will be in four parts.

(a) *Objective tests.* One test to cover each of the topics *(i)*, *(ii)* and *(iv)*. These tests, to be given without warning, will carry a time-limit and no reference books will be available. All three tests will be carried out during the pupil's fifth year.

(b) *An essay.* To be written during the fifth year, relating to some aspect of topic *(v)*. Pupils will be given a list of 'subjects' from which their choice must be made.

(c) *Computer programs.* A folder of computer programs as specified in topic *(iii)*. These programs may be written at any time during the course, and must be accompanied by flowcharts and full documentation.

(d) *Project work.* Towards the end of their fifth year pupils will undertake individually one major study. This may be the writing of a computer program (of greater complexity and sophistication than in *(c)* above); a detailed study of one particular computer installation or a particular application; an investigation of the growth of the computer industry; or the design and construction of simple logic circuits, etc.

The percentage weighting for the assessment will be:

objective tests	45	(15 per cent for each test)
essay	15	
computer programs	20	
project work	20.	

A special O-level group for mathematics was formed in the June of the middle year and was taught by the teacher with experience of this examination. The head of department felt that it would be impossible under the present set-up to teach the vast amount of information required for O-level in a mixed-ability group, or to maintain the existing standard of examination success at this level. He felt that the ethos of this particular examination demanded more formal teaching of the lecture/exercise type. The degree of teacher confidence and the department's unwillingness to use children as guinea-pigs in an educational experiment also affected their decision to provide special tuition for O level. The new group was formed mainly on the recommendation of the teachers.

The preparation and organization of material was left to the individual teacher, who followed the outlined scheme and used the materials and resources available. The teachers prepared their work up to half a term in advance, depending on personal preference. All seemed to agree that they needed a week for ideas to germinate before actually writing work schemes. In general, continuity of teacher from year to year ensured continuity of treatment and content. This autonomy placed on the teacher the responsibility of finding the time to track down fruitful mathematical situations and to put them into a form suitable for introduction to a class. This process required preparedness, skill and an awareness of colleagues' successes and failures; discussion was important in this process. Pupils at either end of the ability spectrum were provided for by their class teacher and his materials. All classes were given homework twice a week and in most cases it was a continuation of work done in class.

Teaching models used with mixed-ability classes

A variety of models were in evidence both across classes and within the same class. Pupils were directed to various tasks either by the teacher or by a 'contract'; a choice of worksheets, booklets or textbooks was usually available. The children worked either on their own or in a group. Tasks took the form of investigations, experiments, exercises or projects. Resources included published materials and school-produced duplicated worksheets, booklets, investigation work cards and guidance cards. The published materials included:

Bass, Doris and Farnham, Anne. *Action Mathematics*, Books 1—5. Cassell, 1971—75.

Brayton, Howard. *Topics in Practical Maths*, Books 1—12. James Brodie, Bath, 1968.

Leapfrogs material (see Chapter VIII).

Marjoram, D. T. E. *Mathematics through Experience*, Books 1—5. Blond Educational, 1970—75.

Moakes, A. J. Croome, P. D. and Philips, T. C. *Pattern and Power of Mathematics*, Books 1—7. Macmillan, 1969—71.

Paling, D., Banwell, C. S. and Saunders, K. D. *Making Mathematics*, Books 1—4. Oxford University Press, 1969.

SMP lettered books (see Chapter VIII).

In the classroom, pupils reach different stages according to choice or teacher direction. The teacher helped the pupil to make the choice. He also helped pupils with difficulties, encouraged discussion, marked work and offered extensions. He acted as guide, instructor and initiator. Outside the classroom his role was just as varied. He had to choose topics from the departmental outline, find sources for suitable work and prepare worksheets, bearing in mind difficulties which could arise. In addition to this he had to mark work; re-write worksheets, trying to eliminate difficulties; examine possibilities for extension work; prepare supplementary material and maintain discussion of progress with colleagues.

To meet all these demands a teacher needs to be dedicated. This was one of the three characteristics of the department, flexibility and teacher autonomy being the other two. The success of the scheme relied on the teacher's ability to produce work suitable for his class and their needs. The personalities of the teachers, their self-confidence and the quiet support of the head of department played an important part in the development of their own teaching styles. There was broad agreement on a general philosophy and the teachers were able, through discussion, to benefit from one another's successes, failures, ideas and materials. Each seemed to be aware of the conditions and activities in other lessons. Together they had developed a subtle, indirectly supportive system. Class descriptions follow which illustrate the individual styles of the different teachers.

Teacher 1. Lower year (55 minutes)

The teacher came in and placed the task booklets on a desk. The tasks were 'Introduction to Computer Studies: Computer Programming, or Meet Mini Cecil', 'Flowcharting, or how to organize things into nice simple steps for the computer to work on'. Both of these were school-produced booklets. The latter was simple and had been introduced by the teacher because the former booklet had proved too difficult for some. The booklets were meant to be a 'taster' for, the fourth-year optional course on computing. Also provided was a set of three worksheets, linearly sequenced, called 'Rotations'.

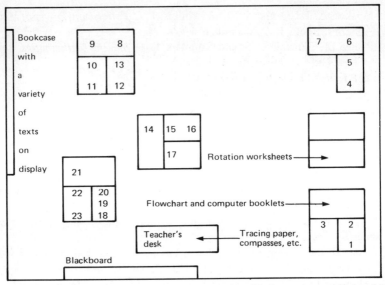

Fig. 4 Seating arrangement and materials for third-year lesson (School B)

The pupils came in, retrieved worksheets or booklets they had started the previous lesson and began to organize themselves. The teacher interrupted to tell them of the alternative booklet for the work on computers. Figure 4 shows the seating arrangement for the lesson, with pupils working in small groups or individually. The twenty-three pupils were engaged in the following tasks:

1
   Flowcharting
2

3 Computer programming

4 The teacher had given them supplementary work to do on measuring
5 angles and using a protractor from *Topics in Practical Maths*, Book 7:
6 Drawing Stars, p. 5, because they had had difficulties with the rotation

116

7	Rotations 1
8	Flowcharting
9	
10	Rotations 3
11	
12	Writing a programme from the computer programming booklet with
13	the help of another teacher in another room.
14	
15	Flowcharting
16	
17	Rotations 3
18	Flowcharting
19	Rotations 2
20	Flowcharting
21	
22	Rotations 2
23	Rotations 1

The pupils appeared to be highly motivated and the classroom was characterized by a calm, business-like atmosphere. Relationships between pupils and between teacher and pupils were friendly and co-operative. Small groups discussed among themselves what they were doing. The teacher went round the class marking, helping, asking questions and making suggestions. The pupils listened patiently to him and he in turn was patient with them. The geography of the classroom allowed for easy movement and discussion. The teacher spent his time approximately in the following proportions:

50 per cent	marking and helping pupils who had asked for assistance,
45 per cent	asking questions, offering suggestions,
5 per cent	administration and organization of materials and pupils.

Teacher 2. Lower year (55 minutes)

The pupils were using a 'contract' system which offered a collection of activities with an element of free choice built in. During the year the pupils had worked from the contracts below. Each contract contained two basic topics (asterisked) which the teacher expected all the pupils to complete during the course of study. Theoretically pupils could choose what they wanted to do in any order. In practice they seemed to complete the two basic topics before choosing any of the others. The free-choice topic could not be done until the pupil had completed two of the other topics.

Contract A
1. Directed numbers*
2. Networks*
3. Statistics
4. Topic work (free choice)
5. More directed numbers
6. Approximating and estimating

Contract B
1. Algebra*
2. Vectors*
3. Investigations
4. Pythagoras
5. Gradient
6. 'Trains and Boats and Planes' (school-produced booklet)
7. Topics (free choice)

Contract C
1. Statistics*
2. Computing ('Computer Programming, or Meet Mini Cecil')*
3. Sets ($\{\ \}$, $\cap$, $\cup$, ϕ, etc.)
4. Topics (free choice)
5. 'Fractions — not ½ easy' (school-produced booklet).

Pupils seemed to consult the teacher for this free-choice topic. The teacher would find out whether the pupils had had difficulties with a particular topic or had found an interesting topic they would like to pursue further. On the basis of this discussion the teacher would offer guidance. A variety of work cards, booklets and texts were available for this work.

Tasks for the lesson were presented in the form of cards, sheets, booklets or texts. Those used for Contract C were:

Statistics

Eight different experiments on separate school-produced worksheets (e.g. measuring the heights, weights, handspans of classmates).

Computing

School-produced booklet.

(These two topics were 'tasters' for the options available in the fourth year.)

Sets

Tasks on four assignment cards:

Card S1: a booklet of simple revision exercises.

Card S2: a booklet of further revision exercises.

Card S3: *Action Mathematics* (Cassell)

    Book 1 (pp. 64–7)

    Book 2 (pp. 64–5)

    Book 3 (pp. 46–8)

    Book 4 (pp. 1–2)

    Book 5 (pp. 62–3)

    Book 6 (pp. 28–31)

Card S4: SMP *Book E*

    Exercise A: Q. 1, 2, 3, 4, 8, 10 (p. 29)

    Exercise B: Q. 1, 5, 6, 7, 8, 9 (p. 32)

Pupils marked their own work.

Topics

A variety of sources.

Fractions

A set of worksheets.

All pupils were encouraged to mark their own work. Answers might be on an answer sheet, on the next sheet or in a textbook. Some questions were left for the teacher to mark; this acted as a check. The teacher collected the pupils' exercise books once a week to make general comments on progress and difficulties. He kept a record of the number of the topic which they were doing and wrote encouraging comments in their books.

On completion of a particular topic the pupil was invited to write a report on that activity. The teacher described the writing of the report as a 'consumer exercise': 'It stops them, they have to look back at what they've done and then say whether they've enjoyed it and why. The purpose is *not* to get them to sum up, rather to get them to give some idea of the quality and suitability of the exercise.' This is a typical pupil's report on graphs and mappings:

> This work was quite difficult and I found that it was quite interesting as well. I like it when the work is not so long and is split up into smaller pieces of work. If a chapter is very long you tend to get bored with the work. It took me a long while to get used to the system. I did not like the homeworks when we did something which had no connection with the work we were doing in class but liked the homework set on graphs. One different homework per week was quite adequate.

The 'contract' system seemed to offer pupils the chance to pursue suitable work and maintained a kind of freshness: there was always something new for them to do. Able pupils were stretched with supplementary work and the less able seemed to be catered for within the two basic topics. The system relied very heavily on teacher intervention and developed the pupils' responsibility for organizing their own work.

During a lesson based on this contract system, the teacher spent his time in the following way:

40 per cent	helping and answering questions
40 per cent	asking questions, demanding explanations
10 per cent	introducing work/homework
10 per cent	administration.

The teacher circulated round the room and gave help to those who asked for it or discovered those who needed assistance. The last ten minutes were spent discussing the previous week's homework, which had been a problem on gambling. Two features became apparent:

i there was little discussion between pupils compared with the lesson of Teacher 1;

ii pupils were unable to explain the rationale of their particular choice of activity.

Teacher 3. Upper year, CSE Mode III (55 minutes)

Before the lesson began the teacher had set out the materials at the front. On arrival, the twenty-seven pupils helped themselves to the appropriate materials.

The pupils' work was based on a 'spiralling' curriculum being developed by the teacher. The content of a 'course', planned to last about half a term, was divided into three main topics and each topic was subdivided into six levels of difficulty. Worksheets were produced for each topic at each level. Pupils could work through the material either remaining within one topic and proceeding through the difficulty levels, or by working from topic to topic at comparable levels of difficulty. Two possible paths are shown in Figure 5. Pupils could choose any path through the scheme on the basis of their own needs and interests.

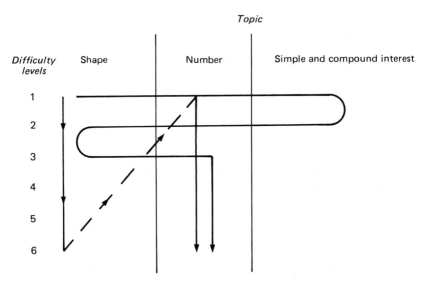

Fig. 5 Work based on a spiralling curriculum

During the lesson the activities were distributed about the class in the following way:

Shape
Seven pupils doing work on areas.

Number
Two pupils doing an investigation on Pascal's Triangle using Paling, Banwell and Saunders' *Making Mathematics*, pp. 40–51.

121

Simple and compound interest
Eighteen pupils doing commercial arithmetic on mortgages, bank loans and savings.

The pattern of each worksheet was: explanation – questions – directions to tasks from other sources, with a measure of choice. The period of time spent by a pupil on each was in general about two weeks; at the end of each task the pupil's work was collected and assessed by the teacher. The teacher was flexible in his approach and demands in order to encourage each pupil to gain as much as possible from each worksheet. Within this scheme a wide range of interests and abilities seemed adequately catered for; even some obviously 'difficult' boys appeared to show interest. Pupils tended to work in pairs and the teacher circulated, discussing work with pupils and encouraging exchanges between pupils. In the observed lesson the teacher spent his time as follows:

50 per cent helping pupils with difficulties;
50 per cent discussing, questioning, offering suggestions, evaluating pupils' progress in order to direct them to the next piece of work.

Teacher 4. Middle year, mixed ability

Worksheets previously prepared by the teacher were put out on the front desk before the lesson began. The pupils,who had been pursuing the topic on chance for a week, came in, helped themselves and started work (for layout of room and distribution of work see Fig. 6). The teacher and a sixth-form pupil acting as a 'floater' circulated answering questions and offering advice. The scheme of work followed the pattern of a main theme, ideas for continuation and supplementary themes.

Main theme
1 Chance (dice etc.)
2 Cricket (WLD etc.); the original worksheet, 'Random Choice', had been replaced since it was too difficult.
3
and How many ways? (ordered pairs)
4

Ideas for continuation
1 Random numbers: *Making Mathematics*, Book 4 (pp. 73–8).
2 Expanding brackets (for potential O-level candidates): *Mathematics through Experience,* Book 3 (p.7).

3 Fishing
(a sampling bottle, a box of beads and a worksheet are needed).

4 Leapfrogs work for the less able: *Networks* 'Chance' and 'Moves'.

The expanded form of idea 2 above was intended to provide a common thread for the more able. This work was a continuous theme, intended to run parallel to the main course, and was completed in a separate exercise book:

multiplying brackets
inequalities and regions
graphs
factorization
curve sketching

permutations and combinations
using algebra
(problem-solving, graphs, etc.)

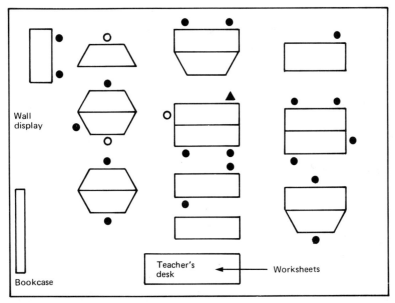

● Probability (Chance worksheets)
○ Expanding brackets (*Mathematics through Experience*, Book 3)
▲ Problems on algebra (*Pattern and Power*, Book 6)

Fig. 6 Layout of room and distribution of work for fourth-year lesson (School B)

Work was written into loose-leaf files, marked and then stored as course-work by the teacher.

The pupils were given continuation work according to their needs and interests. By mutual agreement they were allowed to follow up other topics when they had exhausted the topic on chance (or it had exhausted them).

The teacher spent his time in the following way:

50 per cent	answering questions, giving help and advice;
40 per cent	marking work;
10 per cent	organizing equipment

Discussions in the classroom

One of the strengths of the school was the variety of both materials and teaching models. Flexible groupings had been established in each class according to the needs of the pupils. All teachers encouraged discussions in the classroom; this was a consistent feature of all lessons seen in the school.

Teacher—pupil discussions took the following forms:

a assessment of pupils' work, especially the understanding of what had to be done;

b evaluation of material and the pupils' reaction to it;

c discovering the needs of pupils and the diagnosis of individual difficulties;

d discovering the interests of the pupils;

e encouraging pupils to express themselves mathematically;

f encouraging pupils to write an accurate description of an activity.

Items b, c, and d had a direct bearing on the guidance offered by the teacher to help the pupil make a choice.

All the teachers tried to initiate some exchanges between pupils, but the extent of these discussions in class varied from teacher to teacher. Discussions centred round the following issues;

i hypothesis-testing;

ii checking results;

iii co-operation in statistical surveys;

iv help of a practical nature (e.g. use of a protractor), explanation of concepts, writing up activities;

v making joint decisions about strategies;

vi formulating suitable questions to ask the teacher;

vii discussion of a social nature;

During the working group's survey it was unusual to overhear pupils discussing their work. This was not so in School C. The following fifteen-minute discussion occurred and involved trial and error developing into hypothesis-testing by an iterative process. The pupils had been offered no rules or guidance and the exchanges were entirely pupil initiated. It is interesting to spot the dominant characters in the group.

Three girls were trying to find the centre of rotation of two flags by using tracing paper and compass point. They had traced flag F and were trying to superimpose it on flag F^1 by testing different centres of rotation. There was silence as the girls — Gill (G), Kay (K) and Joanna (J) — tried out different points.

K 'That won't work!'
  (Long pause.)
K 'Sir!'
  (The teacher (T) starts to move towards the group but decides to open a window as the room is rather stuffy; a boy then diverts his attention.)
G 'Have you done it yet?'
K 'No!'
G 'Yes, it's hard isn't it?'
  (The teacher returns. Joanna is not happy with trial and error; it is taking her too long.)
G 'Sir, you know this one . . .' (She puts the compass on the table in frustration.)

125

T (Patiently) 'Well, experiment. Get a compass point, dig it in somewhere and turn the tracing paper. You'll have to experiment more.'

J (In a resigned tone) 'OK.'
   (Silence. Plenty of industry.)

K 'There's so many holes in my tracing paper I think I'm going to run out.'

G (Suddenly) 'I've got it!'

K 'Where?'

G 'It's somewhere along that line. Look . . .'

J 'Yes, I've found it . . . THERE!'
   (She marks the point triumphantly.)

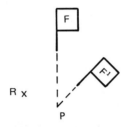

(She marks the centre of rotation R, thinks, then extends the poles of the flags to meet at P.)

J 'Hey, that doesn't follow!' (She points to P.) 'This isn't the centre.'

K 'What's the angle?'

J 'Which angle? Let's join up some lines.'

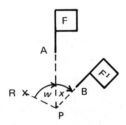

(She takes out a protractor and starts measuring angles.)

K 'That's 90° (she indicates angle RPB).

J 'No it's . . . 115°' (She turns to G.) 'Do you agree with Kay?'

G 'Yes . . . uh . . . No!'
   (Joanna repeats the exercise and measures the angle again.)

J 'There! It's still not 90°!'

K 'Can I borrow your protractor, Jo?'
  (She measures the angle.) 'OK. Yes, I was quite a bit out.'
  (Pause.)
J 'These two angles should be the same but they're not.'
  (She points to angles w and x.)
K 'Why should they be?'
J 'I don't know. I just think they should be.'
  (J then rubs out her working on the paper.)
J 'I think I'll start again and measure the lines and see what they are.'

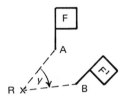

(She measures them and finds RA = 5 cm and RB = 5.2 cm.)
'Blast, it's just over! They must be the same.'
(She gets a new piece of paper and tracing paper and does the whole construction again.)
'Yes, they are!'
(She measures angle y and finds it to be 45°.)
'I've found the centre of rotation, but I want to find out more now I've done it.'
K 'Why don't you try joining some other points?'
  (Joanna joins RC and RD, measures angle z.)

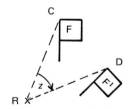

J 'This is $45°$ – the same. I thought it would be.'
  (She turns to Kay) 'Measure yours, see if you get any different.'
  (The teacher comes over and speaks to Joanna.)
T 'What have you been looking at?'
J 'Just my curiosity. I wanted to find the centre of rotation, and then something about it.'

Choice in the classroom

Although this varied from teacher to teacher it was found to be a great motivating factor for both teacher and pupil. The different types of pupil choice have already been outlined in the class descriptions. To summarize:

a Choice from three or four topics. The activities differed in terms of difficulty, that is to say they were not parallel. Within the choice of topics there were one or two tasks which all pupils had to do. There was also some choice within some other topics.

b Free choice was used to develop work and interests, to provide remedial help or to tackle completely new problems. This relied a great deal on teacher guidance and advice; more often than not the more able were encouraged to pursue a particular theme.

With such a degree of teacher autonomy, teacher choice was also of great importance. Pupils were often unable to explain the rationale of their choice and frequently asked the teacher for guidance. One the whole, pupils seemed to find it stimulating to be in an atmosphere where different activities were being pursued at the same time.

Methods of assessment

Assessment was mainly impressionistic, although some tests were taken in the fourth year in an attempt to spot O-level potential. The following were being assessed: achievement, attitude (towards a particular piece of work), amount of work done, presentation and style. There seemed to be no consistency between teachers in the kind of assessments they made or their records; however, they all relied a great deal on discussion with the pupils in making their judgements.

Summary

The characteristic of this school was its sensitivity to the individual needs, interests and abilities of pupils. The following factors influenced the achievement of this aim.

a The social conscience of the teachers.

b The flexibility offered and the way it is used.

c The developing aspect of discussion (the geography of the room was important in encouraging this).

d Teacher autonomy.

e Familiarity of the teacher with his material.

f Ability of the teachers to write their own worksheets and material.

g The head of department's subtle influence; his quiet approval.

h Good motivation of pupils; their encouraging response in turn boosted the morale of the teachers.

i Teacher morale was high.

VIII. Materials in use

This chapter contains descriptive reviews of some publications, materials and schemes which were in use in the survey schools visited by members of the working group. It also contains details of local collaborative activities encountered and professional associations which can offer help. Further details may be obtained from publishers, project headquarters or the addresses given.

ASSOCIATION OF TEACHERS OF MATHEMATICS

Market Street Chambers, Nelson, Lancashire BB9 7LN

Pamphlets with material suitable for mixed-ability classes are available from the Association. These include:

Pegboard Games
(Suitable for group activity.)

Sticks
(A collection of ideas and starting points for the secondary classroom.)

Geoboards
(Another collection of ideas.)

Turning the Tables
(Some number situations for children in the primary or lower secondary school.)

Numbers Everywhere
(Number situations for the secondary classroom.)

Pegboards
(Activities for children.)

Fifteen Starters for the Secondary Classroom
(A variety of situations suitable for the secondary school.)

Rods, Blocks and Balances
(Workbook for teachers of 8—13-year-olds using coloured rods, Unifix cubes and equalizers.)

Ideas for Slow Learners
(Two pamphlets containing a collection of ideas for use with slow learners in secondary schools.)

ATM have also published *Mixed Ability Groups No. 1* (1973), which is about the teaching of mathematics to mixed-ability groups in secondary schools. It consists of a number of personal accounts based on experience in a variety of different situations.

Each member of the Association receives a copy of the quarterly journal *Mathematics Teaching*, which often contains articles and reviews relevant to mixed-ability teaching. The Association has sponsored conferences and meetings at local branch level when the theme has been the teaching of mathematics to mixed-ability groups. During the annual conference, seminars are held to discuss issues associated with teaching such groups.

DEVELOPMENT OF IDEAS IN MATHEMATICAL EDUCATION (DIME) PROJECTS

Department of Education, University of Stirling, Scotland

This project has produced a range of *Mathematics Workcard Booklets* with associated worksheets and equipment. These booklets were originally designed as part of the Fife Mathematics Project for mixed-ability classes in Fife comprehensive schools. Each booklet contains eight work cards on a specific topic and booklets follow each other in ascending order of difficulty. Booklets are grouped in the following series:

3D Sketching (Booklets 11—15)
(Develops the ability to interpret and draw isometric sketches; extends activities to simple transformations.)

Operations (21 and 22)
(A diagrammatic approach to linear functions which introduces algebraic notation as a way of describing simple mappings.)

Shapes (31–33)
(Simple shapes and their classifications.)

Number mappings (41 and 42)
(Representing linear mappings.)

Angles (51)
(Develops the concept in a practical way.)

Number patterns (61 and 62)
(Algebraic notation is used in their description and generalization.)

Area (71–73)
(A study of various shapes including geoboard polygons.)

Motion geometry (81)
(Symmetry through the use of a mirror.)

After further revision in the light of classroom experience, the booklets will be published by Oliver & Boyd. Various other materials are also available. Further details of this scheme may be obtained from the project director at the above address.

HERTFORDSHIRE COMPUTER MANAGED MATHEMATICS PROJECT

The Advisory Unit for Computer Based Education, 19 St Albans Road, Hatfield, Hertfordshire

HCMMP is an all-ability worksheet-based course for 11–13-year-old pupils. The three components of the course are available separately and consist of:

> Twenty-five modules of work, each usually consisting of twelve worksheets, a studysheet and ancillary material. Each module is divided into four or five levels of difficulty (A–E). All children begin at A and work through the levels. Each level of difficulty is subdivided into three worksheets: 'M', 'T' and 'X'. The 'M' and 'X' sheets are submitted on mark-sensed documents or cards and are marked by computer. The 'X' sheet is designed for extra practice and pupils are assigned to it according to their performance on the 'M' sheet. The 'T' sheet is teacher marked and allows for more flexible activities.

Twenty-four videotaped programmes, each 15–20 minutes long, used to introduce a module.

Computer software to mark pupils' work, schedule pupils on to fresh work and to provide teacher registers and analyses for pupil performance.

Further details are available from the director at the above address.

KENT MATHEMATICS PROJECT

This Kent Curriculum Project was set up under the auspices of the Kent Education Authority in 1966. In 1976–77 the Schools Council funded the development of additional material for the very slow learner at secondary level. Teaching materials from the project are to be published by Ward Lock Educational. The aims of the project were:

a To provide a unique course in mathematics for each individual child, using material suitable for all abilities of children between 9 and 16 years and tailored to pupils' weaknesses and special interests.

b To provide teachers with a flexible system within which they can, if they desire, introduce their own interests and skills.

c To give the teacher opportunities to use his or her skills at diagnosing weaknesses, helping children to develop concepts and establishing co-operative rather than teacher-dominated relationships.

d To provide a system in which children will accept responsibility for most of their own learning, not working in isolation but with social interaction with other children.

e To offer an assessment of each pupil's mathematical ability at any stage in his or her learning career, culminating in Mode III CSE or O-level assessments.

The individualized course consists of an entry requirements list; a diagnostic test to be taken on entry; a bank of course material consisting of worksheets, booklets and tapes; a short test for each task; a hierarchical flowchart for the tasks; matrix cards; record cards; teacher's notes; and test answers.

The KMP material bank consists of about 1200 tasks given in about 2000 presentations appropriate to the needs of fast, medium, slow and very slow secondary (L) pupils. The tasks are divided into eight main levels, with an 'overflow' level nine catering for the exceptionally bright 16-year-old. The range of material in the different levels is:

Levels 1–3 (Primary)
from fast 8–11-year-olds to slow 11-year-olds

Levels 1–3 (Secondary)
slow and very slow 12–16-year-olds

Levels 4–6 (CSE)
from slow 15–16-year-olds to fast 11–13-year-olds

Levels 6–9 (O level)
from average 15–16-year-olds to fast 13–16-year-olds.

Each level is subdivided into five parts, and a flowchart of tasks is constructed for the scheme as a whole. By using fast, medium and slow codes, material can be identified as being suitable for different children. Where there are alternative sheets for the same task this is also shown on the flowchart. The teacher uses the flowchart and the pupil's past performance to assign the child's matrix of eleven tasks. The working procedure is shown in Table 3.

Table 3 Working procedure for course based on KMP materials

Pupil	Teacher
Take entry test	
	Mark entry test and use results to select entry matrix.
Complete matrix tasks in any order. Mark own work.	Make alternative choices if tasks do not suit the pupil. Check and sign off tasks. Help when necessary.
Take matrix test.	
Free choice.	Mark matrix test and use results to make new matrix from the flow diagram.
Start new matrix.	
	Keep records.

LEAPFROGS

Coldharbour, Newton St Cyres, Exeter, Devon

Books in the *Network* series are in general published by Hutchinson for the Leapfrogs Group (though some material is issued by the group themselves – see below). The books in the series are conceived for use with mixed-ability classes of 10–14-year-old pupils and are designed to provide ideas and activities to stimulate the learner's involvement in mathematics. Three kinds of books are available:

Action books
Booklets on particular themes which invite the reader to explore the consequences of specific actions. Titles include *Animations, Bands, Chance, Codes, Cubes, Doodles, Folds, Moves, Orders, Pegboards, Prints* and *Tiles* (1975–76).

Links
Anthologies of pictures and diagrams to stimulate a variety of possible mathematical reactions: *Links, Leads* and *Leaves* (1975–76).

With Few Words
Work books which introduce some basic mathematical ideas through puzzles, diagrams and drawings: *Blue Book, Orange Book* and *Green Book* (1975–76).

Other material has been produced by the group. This includes a cassette tape recording, 8mm films, large posters and packs of slides. Further details may be obtained from the above address.

MATHEMATICAL ASSOCIATION
259 London Road, Leicester LE2 3BE

The fundamental aim of the Mathematical Association is to promote good methods of mathematics teaching. The Association has differing grades of membership, enabling members to receive some or all of its publications. These publications are *Mathematics in School* (issued five times a year), which sometimes contains articles and reviews concerned with teaching mathematics to mixed-ability groups, and *The Mathematical Gazette* (four issues a year) containing articles and reviews of a more specialized nature, reports on various aspects of the teaching of mathematics and the Association's *Newsletter*, which gives other up-to-date information. The Association sponsors conferences and meetings at national and local level and its branches hold meetings at which mixed-ability teaching of mathematics has been a theme. During the annual national conference a working group meets to discuss this issue. Its teaching committee has sub-committees, one of which (the 9–16 age range sub-committee) investigated and issued an informal report on mixed-ability teaching in 1974/75. The Association's revised guide to *Mathematics Projects in British Secondary Schools* (Bell, 1976) contains information about many schemes used with mixed-ability classes. *Why, What and How*, dealing with some aspects related to mixed-ability teaching, was published by the Association in 1976.

MATHEMATICS FOR THE MAJORITY CONTINUATION PROJECT

Schools Council project, 1971–75, directed by Peter Kaner and Norman Pass.

This Schools Council project provides a variety of material for pupils of up to average ability in the 13–16 age range and these have been incorporated into mixed-ability schemes such as SMILE (see below). Four packs of MMCP teaching materials have been published for the Council by Schofield & Sims, each pack being based around an environmental theme:

> *Buildings* (1974)
> *Communication* (1974)
> *Travel* (1975)
> *Physical Recreation* (1975)

Each pack contains approximately fifteen wallets and each wallet contains assignments on the theme in the form of work cards and booklets. The supporting material includes information cards, games and practical materials. There is a teacher's handbook in each pack, which includes notes and advice on how to use and develop the material.

136

MODULAR MATHEMATICS ORGANIZATION

Modular Mathematics (Heinemann Educational Books, 1975).

This course is designed to provide a core of content for all pupils in the 11–13 age range, with supplementary material for the more able and special provision for the less able pupils. The thirty-six modules are grouped in cycles, each cycle containing four modules. Pupils complete the work in cycles. Each module develops a mathematical topic and provides an average of 6–8 hours work by means of work cards, worksheets and a set of apparatus. Two sets of teacher's notes, answers and an example book (one set for each year of the course) are also provided.

The work cards and worksheets are colour coded according to the level of difficulty. The red and orange sets provide the core for each module.

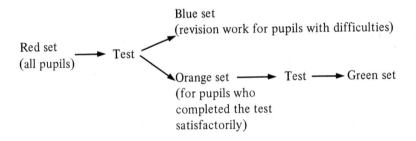

OXFORD COMPREHENSIVE MATHEMATICS

D. Paling and M. E. Wardle, *Oxford Comprehensive Mathematics*, Books 1 and 2 (Oxford University Press, 1975).

These books are designed specifically for use with mixed-ability classes. As each topic is introduced, activities, ideas and computation appropriate to three levels of thinking are given. These levels are clearly indicated along the exercises by a colour coding.

OXFORD MATHEMATICS GROUP

Resource Mathematics, Units 1–3 (John Murray, 1976).

This is a scheme written by the mathematics staff of Chipping Norton School and is designed for first-year mixed-ability classes. Fifteen topics are presented in three books of spirit masters with five topics in each book. For example, Unit 2 contains symmetry, number, relations, number bases and fractions. Within each topic there are three categories of worksheets: 'A' sheets present core work for all pupils, 'B' sheets are designed for the top two-thirds of the ability range and 'C' sheets provide extension work for the top third. Each unit also contains a pupils' study book, which summarizes each topic, and teacher's notes which give details of strategies, materials, apparatus and answers.

RESOURCES FOR LEARNING DEVELOPMENT UNIT (RFLDU) MATHEMATICS PROJECT

Redcross Street, Bristol BS2 OBA

Independent learning materials produced at the Unit so far have been written by many teachers for children in the first two years of secondary school. It is not a course but a collection of resources in the form of small booklets, worksheets and games organized under topic headings. The content covered is that which is frequently taught in the first years of secondary schools. There are materials in the collection suitable for children of widely differing abilities; the level of difficulty of each item is indicated by a code.

Further details and catalogues are available from the above address.

SCHOOL MATHEMATICS PROJECT

The Main School Course, Books A–H, Cards I and II (Cambridge University Press, 1973–74).

The cards are designed as an alternative, more flexible treatment of the mathematics in the *Main School Course*, Books A, B, C and D. Cards I are subdivided into three packs: the main pack, used by most pupils most of the time; a preliminary pack for pupils who need to do preparatory work in particular topics, often providing basic number work; and the supplementary pack, containing some harder work and enrichment material. The main pack is arranged into topics which are in turn subdivided as shown in the flow diagram below.

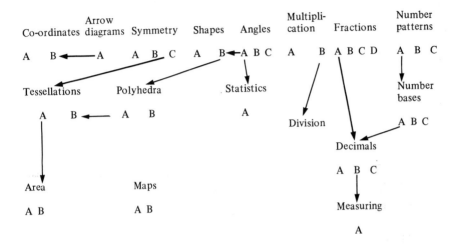

The topics are subdivided into thirty-eight sections with about seven cards to a section. There are eight possible starter sets of cards and these are shown in the top line of the flow diagram. Each sequence of cards is followed by a check card and test card. Teacher's notes are included and a pack of stencils is also available for the various duplicated sheets required for use with the cards.

SECONDARY MATHEMATICS INDIVIDUALIZED LEARNING EXPERIMENT (SMILE)

Developed by the Inner London Education Authority at Ladbroke Mathematics Centre, Middle Row School, Kensal Road, London W10 5DB

SMILE is an individualized learning situation developed from KMP (see above) for use with mixed-ability classes. It aims to provide a learning situation suited to each pupil's ability and experience with an emphasis on the pupil's learning rather than the teacher's teaching. It uses the following resources:

139

a task cards and commercial material, hierarchically structured;
b answer books and test books;
c equipment needed for a particular task;
d the teacher.

Material is written by the teachers and regular meetings are held to discuss progress at Ladbroke Mathematics Centre.*

THE SOUTH NOTTINGHAMSHIRE PROJECT

A. W. Bell, D. Rooke, and A. R. Wigley, *The South Nottinghamshire Project, Report 1973–75*, Notes, Material and Commentary (University of Nottingham, School of Education, Shell Centre for Mathematical Education, 1975).

This project accepts the principle of the whole class working in the same general field but with differentiation of the particular problems attempted by individuals. It rejects individualized, independent learning schemes as a strategy for teaching mixed-ability classes.

Two essential arguments concerning the mathematical education of 11–12-year-old pupils are incorporated into the scheme. Firstly that pupils should investigate mathematics for themselves, leading to the drawing of conclusions, the making of generalizations and the giving of explanations and proofs. Secondly that simple apparatus provides the best means of entry into mathematical activity at this age.

The material is a deliberate attempt to provide situations to which every pupil can respond at whatever level is valid for him. The content is based on fourteen topics, each of two and half weeks duration. These include statistics, whole number relationships, shape, symmetry, angle, binary numbers, sequences and functions, decimals, tessellations, functions and graphs, fractions and ratio, area and topology. For each topic there are background notes, a general survey of possible content, work cards and a teacher's commentary. The teacher's commentary contains details of materials needed, the main content and process objectives, a description of the significance of the topic, lesson introductions, suggestions for helping the least able and extensions for the more able.

Each topic begins with a situation discussed by the teacher with the class; the investigation is then continued by the pupils (see Fig. 7). The teacher gives

*For a full account of this local collaborative activity, see R. Gibbons, 'An account of the Secondary Mathematics Individualized Learning Experiment', *Mathematics in School*, vol. 4 (6) November 1975.

extension questions to different groups of pupils as and when they are ready, either orally or on cards.

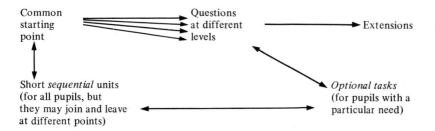

Fig. 7 The South Nottinghamshire Project: elements in investigation of a topic

The project stresses the need to avoid swamping the teacher with low-level work: marking, testing, organizing work cards, but instead to free him for the important tasks: initiating work, stimulating discussions and intervening to suggest new problems. It aims to offer flexibility, providing sufficient guidance for beginners and non-specialist teachers, without demanding a rigid or whole-hearted commitment to the materials.

THE STRUCTURED MATHEMATICS SCHEME

Structured Mathematics Centre, Reaside School, Rea Street South, Birmingham B5 6LB

Ostensibly this scheme was designed to produce materials for those teachers who are not mathematics specialists. Work takes the form of mathematics packages devoted to single topics. Each package contains enough worksheets for thirty children for 10–15 lessons; a teacher's handbook containing notes on how to use the material and answers; a post-test matched to the objectives listed in the teacher's handbook, and, where appropriate, a pre-test. Some of the material is available to teachers outside Birmingham and further details may be obtained from the director.

FURTHER MATERIALS

C. Banwell, K. Saunders, and D. Tahta, *Starting Points* (Oxford University Press, 1972)

In chapter II a selection of mathematical situations which may be used as starting points for further investigations are discussed. Most of these situations can be developed with mixed-ability classes. This text has proved a useful handbook for teachers considering mixed-ability teaching in mathematics. It discusses many aspects relevant to this kind of teaching including topics such as the role of the teacher, work cards, write-ups, assessments, projects, using resources and the use of various materials.

D. S. Fielker, and J. Mold, *Topics from Mathematics* (Cambridge University Press, 1967–75)

A series of booklets suitable for individual and group work with a wide scope for extended independent study. Titles include *Computers, Statistics, Cubes, Towards Probability, Circles, Solid Models, Tessellations, Triangles, Rolling and Number Lines.*

Acknowledgements

The working group wishes to acknowledge the co-operation of those who willingly gave us so much help in carrying out our survey and in compiling this report.

We should particularly like to thank those advisers who replied to our initial inquiry and the many teachers who provided useful information and comments.

We are also grateful to those who received and helped us on our visits to survey schools. Many have given permission for teaching notes, worksheets, records and other material to be reproduced here and we gladly acknowledge the invaluable assistance thus afforded. It should be established that the schools may not necessarily agree with the way the evidence is presented, or with the conclusions drawn, since they will not have had the opportunity of seeing the report before it was published.

The survey schools, with their age range in parentheses, are listed below:

Belper High School (13–18), Derbyshire
Brislington School (11–18), Bristol

The Castle School (11–18), Thornbury, Bristol
Cheshunt School (11–18), Waltham Cross, Hertfordshire
Chipping Norton School (11–18), Oxfordshire
Crown Woods School (11–18), London SE9

David Lister High School (13–18), Hull

The Hedley Walter School (11–18), Brentwood, Essex
Holland Park School (11–18), London W8
Holly Lodge High School (11–16), Smethwick, Warley, West Midlands
Horsforth School (11–18), Leeds

John Smeaton High School (13–18), Leeds
John Smeaton Middle School (9–13), Leeds

Kibworth High School (11—14), Leicestershire

Longbenton High School (13—18), Newcastle upon Tyne

Radyr Comprehensive School (11—18), Cardiff
Ridgewaye School (11—16), Tunbridge Wells, Kent
Rushcliffe Comprehensive School (11—18), West Bridgford, Nottinghamshire

Settle High School (13—18), North Yorkshire
Slatyford School (11—18), Newcastle upon Tyne
South Wolds Comprehensive School (11—18), Keyworth, Nottinghamshire

Thomas Telford High School (11—16), West Bromwich, West Midlands
Town Centre Comprehensive School (11—18), Sutton-in-Ashfield, Nottinghamshire

Wickersley High School (11—18), South Yorkshire
The Woodlands Comprehensive School (11—18), Coventry, West Midlands
Wyndham School (11—18), Egremont, Cumbria

Although not part of the survey, the following schools were also visited briefly to gather information:

Backwell School (11—18), Bristol

Christchurch Secondary School for Girls (11—16), Chatham, Kent
Christopher Wren School (11—18), London W12

North Farm Middle School (9—13), Leeds

Thornhill Middle School (9—13), Leeds

Whalley Range High School for Girls (11—18), Manchester

We were grateful for the efficient secretarial work and typing of Mrs E. Hale and Mrs B. Rose and the facilities and help offered at Brigshaw Comprehensive School, Leeds, in the preparation of all the interim documents associated with the work of the group. We would also like to acknowledge the advice and help of the Schools Council's Publications Section. Finally, we would like to thank our curriculum officer at the Council for her guidance, contributions and patient support and Mr P. A. Bailey, the secretary/writer to the group, without whose dedication and commitment it would not have been possible to produce this report.

Members of the working group

R. T. Richardson (Chairman)	Deputy Headteacher, Chelmer Valley High School, Chelmsford, Essex
A. G. Ahmed	Head of Mathematics Department, Fairchildes High School, New Addington, London Borough of Croydon
J. Bancroft	Head of Mathematics Department, Westfield School, Bedford
Dr A. W. Bell	Senior Lecturer, Shell Centre for Mathematical Education, University of Nottingham
M. J. Cahill	Deputy Headteacher, Frank F. Harrison School, Walsall, West Midlands
R. H. H. Corke	Head of Mathematics Department, Duffryn High School, Newport, Gwent
Mrs P. Fletcher	Head of Mathematics Department, Buckpool School, Stourbridge, West Midlands
Miss R. Gibbons	Deputy Warden, Ladbroke Mathematics Centre, London W10
B. J. Goacher	Research Officer, National Foundation for Educational Research
D. S. Hale (until September 1976)	Lecturer, Shell Centre for Mathemcatical Education, University of Nottingham

J. W. Hersee	Executive Director, The School Mathematics Project, Westfield College, University of London (Chairman, Schools Council Mathematics Committee, from September 1977)
D. M. J. Hockley	Headteacher, Yew Tree High School, Manchester
D. W. Lingard	Director of Studies, Belper High School, Derbyshire
G. W. Rodda	Senior Adviser, Knowsley Metropolitan Borough Education Department, Huyton, Liverpool
P. A. Bailey (Secretary/writer)	Schools Council (seconded from the post of Head of Mathematics, Brigshaw Comprehensive School, Leeds
Mrs J. A. Denyer	Curriculum Officer, Schools Council

The working group was glad of the availability of HMI Mr T. J. Fletcher for consultation.